Lady Barrett Lennard

Constance Rivers

Lady Barrett Lennard

Constance Rivers

ISBN/EAN: 9783337238254

Printed in Europe, USA, Canada, Australia, Japan

Cover: Foto ©Andreas Hilbeck / pixelio.de

More available books at **www.hansebooks.com**

CONSTANCE RIVERS.

BY

LADY BARRETT LENNARD.

" My fondest—faintest—latest accents hear—
 Grief for the dead not Virtue can reprove;
 Then give me all I ever ask'd—a tear,
 The first—last—sole reward of so much love!"
   The Corsair.

IN THREE VOLUMES.

VOL. II.

LONDON:
HURST AND BLACKETT, PUBLISHERS,
13, GREAT MARLBOROUGH STREET.
1867.

The right of Translation is reserved.

LONDON:
PRINTED BY MACDONALD AND TUGWELL,
BLENHEIM HOUSE.

CHAPTER I.

"When evening descended from heaven above,
And the earth was all red, and the air was all love,
And delight, though less bright, was far more deep,
And the day's veil fell from the world of sleep."
SHELLEY.

FOR several following days Lyla, accompanied by the herdsman, brought milk and honeycomb to Eustace every morning. They staid only a few minutes; and he could not understand why the mother thus officiously ostended the beauties of her daughter.

One night the moon gave by its brilliancy a softer daylight, and Eustace, sleeping in his tent, was awakened by the touch of something smooth, cold, and heavy on his feet. He started up, and saw a white figure drooping over his bed, with dark tresses sweeping over him, which, from their weight and glossiness, gave the feeling of a snake gliding over him. "Lyla!" he exclaimed. She raised her head, and motioned him to silence. Kali Khan slept at no great distance outside the enclosure. She drew near to his face, and seemed ready to whisper into his ear.

"Why art thou come, child of the mountain?" said he. "Why hast thou come at midnight through the shadows and unfrequented paths?"

Lyla seemed indisposed to answer. She only wept, and nestled her head on his breast.

"Thou art mighty, Sahib—mighty to save—thou art like the sun in power—thou art the moon in softness—thou wilt redeem thy slave!"

"Has she beaten thee again?"

Lyla wept.

"Tell me if I can aid thee?"

"I am thine—thy slave without cost—let me be thine own!" and Lyla raised herself from the ground, and seated herself on the edge of the couch. Eustace's arms stole round that lithe form, so soft, so rounded and youthful. His lips were pressed to the dimpled shoulder which came so near his lips.

"Oh! Lyla, why didst thou come to tempt me?"

"Sahib!—let me be thine own!—take me away with thee! I fear thy departure!— I cannot live if thou art away!"

"My child, thou knowest not what thou askest. I am a chief. To my followers I say, I will not that women encumber my camp—they must go. Could I say this and keep thee?"

"Thou art a great Sahib—they may have slaves—little sahibs—not—"

"It must not be," said Eustace, with a great mental effort. "Thou mayst marry a good man, and be a happy mother of children—*I* cannot marry thee!"

"No—not marry!" said the panting girl. "Alas! I am but thy slave; but I cannot be any but thine—and oh! Sahib, they will take me away—they will sell me! My mother thought that Sahib would offer to buy me, but another Sahib saw me on the mountain. He will pay much gold to my mother—but I am thine, oh! my beloved—my soul thirsteth after thee—send me not away!"

He had left her seated on the bed, and she rose and flung herself on her knees before him, embracing his feet.

"Rise, Lyla. Alas! my child, what can I do with thee?"

She sprung to his neck and clung round it.

" Love me !"

When Eustace awoke on the following morning from a deep sleep, he felt a confused hope that he had but dreamed of the visit from Lyla. He was glad to fancy that his evil wishes had conjured up the "phantom of slumber."

He raised his head on his arm, and looked listlessly on the magnificent landscape which the open folds of his tent disclosed; mountains melting into the sky, and touched by the rose hues of early morning; distant groves of rhododendrons, purple with their tufted blossoms, and rivers dashing down between the clefts of the rocks like liquid silver. Nor was the landscape tenantless. Herds of gazelles bounded from rock to rock, or stood quietly feeding in the shadows. The parrots, brilliant in the new-born light, and more voluble from their night's rest, flapped their extended wings and screamed discordant joy amongst their fellows; whilst the peacock reared his graceful neck of blue and gold, and extended his gorgeous plumes to attract the attention of his mate.

The eyes of Eustace ached at the brilliancy of the scene, and sought for rest within the shadow of his tent. What saw he there, which made his heart stop for an instant? It was no bigger than a pin's head, but it betrayed the events of the night —a bit of tinsel broken off from the embroidered scarf of the young Asiatic.

Eustace groaned, and covered his face. Temptation had come, and he had succumbed to it.

What was to become of that passionate girl—so helpless, so ungovernable? He loved her as men love for the first time, with a boy's tenderness—with a man's passion. How different were his present feelings from that fancy for Claudine which had made Lady Yorke so uneasy? How faded now appeared that love, since time had rolled its waves over it—so formidable then—so insignificant now!

Should he throw aside the ambition which had been his idol, and live with this child, like a patriarch, amongst these woodland mountains?

He thought of what his progeny would be, and shuddered—creatures mean, subtile, creeping, degraded, with the vices of both races and the virtues of neither—*half-castes!* Yet, with the thoroughly European horror of half-castes, the proud Anglo-Saxon never stops to consider that to his own sin we owe those defects in the human race.

"What can I do with her?" he repeated

constantly; and each time the question seemed more difficult of solution.

He, the youth hitherto so strong in purpose, was now content to enjoy the present hour, and wilfully to shut his eyes to the future. He was content to be borne along on the smooth stream of pleasure, and to forget that a rapid was near, into which he and the object of his love would be soon precipitated.

He knew she would return on the next night, and lay dreamily awaiting her till he felt the pressure of her lips on his brow. Both slept till the sun had risen on the following morning; and Lyla knew that by that time her mother must have discovered her absence, and she refused to return. Eustace did not urge it; the remembrance of the bruises on her slender arms prevented him.

She lived in his tent; if he walked out,

he always found her on his return seated at the door, her large lustrous eyes intent on the path by which she looked for his coming. It was impossible not to love a creature so beautiful and so devoted; and Eustace's devotion would have satisfied the most unreasonable of divinities. He gave her little save his love and protection—a bit of pierced gold which she wore round her neck, suspended by a chain made of her own hair, and some valuable scarfs which Eustace had used as turbans in his Irregular Cavalry dress. Eustace had but one ornament, a ring, the gift of his mother, and this he would not sacrifice even to Lyla.

They heard nothing of her mother's wrath; and as weeks went onward, they had ceased to dread or to expect it. Eustace and Kali Khan used to leave the tent frequently for hours in their chase of wild animals, with the conviction that the beautiful face of Lyla would be seen shining out clearly and brightly from the background made by the recesses of the tent, whilst the folds fell on each side as a frame-work of the picture.

On the morning of the day on which Lyla had overslept herself, Kali Khan was sent by Eustace to fetch the milk, lest the mother should have a meeting with the delinquent daughter. He did not start till the glass of Eustace had revealed the figure of the woman descending the mountain, and they met where the two ascents were united at their base. Kali received the milk in silence.

"She is in the tent of the Sahib?" said the mother, interrogatively.

Kali gave a syllable of assent.

"It is well!"

This was her only observation as she returned up the mountain.

A childless mother is an object to excite sympathy; but had the workings of that woman's heart been laid open, what a hell would have been revealed! Sometimes a flood of tenderness softened her wild black eyes, as she looked at the empty bed of dried grass and skins. She had ever given her daughter those which were warmest and softest, and had been economical of the annas which the sale of her milk procured, to purchase clothing for her child superior to that of other girls in her daughter's rank of life. Simple ornaments, too, she had obtained, coarsely executed silver ornaments and bracelets, which could not add to the rounded beauty of Lyla's arms, but the glitter of which gratified the semi-savage eyes of her mother. She was ambitious, too, in her own way. She wanted to sell her daughter; but she imagined that in doing this she was ensuring that daughter's wealth and happiness, by placing her in a position superior to that in which she had been born. It was the same feeling which possessed the ambitious mother of Madame Pompadour, who thanked Heaven, on her death-bed, that she could die happy, now that her child was established as the mistress of the king.

The mother of Lyla glared round her deserted den, and, seated on the ground, laid her head on the knees which her wiry arms embraced, and wept aloud in her loneliness. She had had for years no kindred, nothing to bind her to her fellow-creatures but this slight girl, who had drawn her sustenance from her mother's breast when they first retreated to that wild dwelling, and had made part of the widow's existence, till her flight to the tent of Eustace.

Notwithstanding the violence with which

she treated Lyla for small faults, she loved her with a passionate devotion little known in colder climes, and Lyla had responded tenderly to her affection, till the instincts of her untutored nature flung her into the arms of our hero.

He was then everything to the young Asiatic. In the tumults of this first-felt passion, her mother had become to her an object only of fear and avoidance. Lyla would have been glad to fly to the world's end with Eustace, not only to be with him, but to escape from the terrors with which the remembrance of her parent pursued her.

She used to start from sleep, and cling fearfully to the arms of Eustace, believing that she perceived a gigantic figure glaring on her from the shadows of night, and entreated him piteously not to give her up to her mother. But as days lengthened into weeks, and the woman made no effort to repossess herself of her daughter, Lyla regained her tranquillity; and both Eustace and his companion believed that no attempt would be made.

This was the aspect of affairs, when the mother of Lyla met Kali Khan one morning with tears and outcries. A tiger had come in the night and carried off one of the finest of her calves.

"Would not the Sahib pursue the tiger and shoot him?" The Sahib was wise and mighty—he would deliver her from the tiger.

The calf was that animal of roving propensities whose erratic taste had led to the interview between Eustace and Lyla at the foot of the mountain. Had it remained with the rest of the herd, the tiger, being an animal of unbounded stomach, would doubtless have preferred the calf's mother. The idea of a tiger hunt made the heart of Eustace bound with excitement. He had never been intended by nature to pass "the spring of manhood in a myrtle shade;" and after his recent inaction the thought of danger thrilled his breast with rapture.

When Kali Khan hastened back with the intelligence of the calf's abduction to Eustace, the scanty population on the lower part of the mountain accompanied him to learn what the Sahib was going to do towards delivering them from a tyrant whom they would not brave themselves, unaccompanied by a master mind.

As some hours had elapsed before the mother of Lyla had given notice of her loss, the beaters imagined that the tiger had had sufficient time to gorge himself with the carcass of his prey, and to compose himself to sleep afterwards. Heavily flapping wings of vultures were to be observed descending slowly across the clear morning sky, lured by the scent of death towards the spot where remained what the tiger had left of his meal, and the prolonged howl of the jackals made a tocsin to the feast. These sights and sounds indicated where the terrible adversary was to be encountered. Eustace dressed himself in a costume of dark brown, more easily to escape the observation of the wary beast, and seized his arms—his musket and a sharp tulwar.

As he took these, his eyes fell on the upturned face of Lyla—her countenance pallid and expressive of the most intense anxiety. How different were the feelings of the two!—Eustace "hailed in his heart the conquest to come;" Lyla's breast was aching with terror and presentiment of evil. He withdrew her into the tent and embraced her fondly.

"I shall soon return to my love—to my

bosom's queen!" he said. " She shall have the claws of the tiger as a charm to hang round her neck."

She spoke not in reply—she knew remonstrance would be vain—she only clung round his neck for a brief space, and then sunk down on the ground, and hid her face with the folds of the scarf Eustace had given her.

Then he departed, and she rushed to the opening of the tent, to catch the last glimpse of his departing form.

How noble and stately were his movements contrasted with the sinuous gait of the dark lithe figures who ran stooping and eager by his side! Lyla looked with eyes too hot for tears—she felt that she should see him no more!

The spot to which Eustace and the natives were directed by the birds of prey, was a nullah, or deep ravine, through which ran a watercourse; for tigers like to take their meals where they can also slake their thirst. There is a shrub called korinda, which with its dense arching foliage makes a convenient retreat for beasts of prey. Under this shelter, and half buried in the moonje grass, the animal was lying asleep. Standing stealthily at some distance, Eustace observed the wonderful beauty of the creature, as he lay, partly curled round, with his velvet nose and chin resting on his hind leg, very much after the fashion of the cat which thus occupies our hearth-rug. The tiger was clearly striped with black on a tawny ground, and was considered to be an unusually fine specimen.

Eustace and the beaters were on a rock at some distance from his lair, and not sufficiently near to make sure of wounding him mortally if he was fired on from where they stood.

A hurried consultation took place. There was no tree sufficiently high to admit of Eustace's climbing it, and remaining in safety, should the tiger awake. To advance and fire whilst standing on the ground would be to brave certain death.

The natives, with quick yet stealthy movements, erected a scaffolding of bamboo canes, brought for the purpose, which were driven into the soft mud by the side of the water-course. These were tied tightly together, and were about twenty-five feet in height. Eustace climbed to the top of this enclosure, and Kali Khan, after handing him up his gun and tulwar, reluctantly left his master, whilst prayers and good wishes were muttered by the Asiatics, who looked forward with joy to the hope of spoil.

I will not assert that the heart of my hero did not beat faster when he stood on his rickety elevation, and knew that so soon as the tiger awoke he would discover that human pulses were beating in his neighbourhood. He was impatient, however, for action, and shouted to the retreating natives to arouse the enemy so soon as they could with safety to themselves. His orders were soon obeyed. They shouted, they fired guns, rattled stones in metal pots, blew horns, and produced noises so discordant, that the mighty beast was observed to stretch out his velvet paws at right angles from his body, and yawn portentously—so fearful were the teeth disclosed in the movement. In a few moments he arose and shook himself, and, not feeling yet the pangs of hunger, his movements were so deliberate as to increase the nervousness under which Eustace constitutionally suffered.

Presently he became aware of the presence of his human foe, and walked to the enclosure, raising himself on his hind legs, and resting the fore-paws on one of the transverse pieces of bamboo, snuffing with his nose in the air, with an appearance of anticipated relish for his coming meal, which induced Eustace to lose no time. He rested his gun on the ledge on which he stood, and fired. The shock carried the animal rolling backwards, but to recover immediately, burning with rage, and the fury of pain and despair. He flung himself on the slight scaffolding, which rocked and reeled under his weight, and raised himself so high against the bamboo support, that his fore-paw reached the foot of Eustace, who, stooping down, severed the clinging paw at the joint, and made the tiger drop back with a yell of agony.

As he rolled over and over on the grass, Eustace felt convined that though no blood flowed from the wound, which the loose

skin had covered in his movements, his
enemy was mortally wounded, and required
only time to finish the struggle. Still the
beaters and Kali Khan did not approach,
though the tiger had ceased to lash his
flexile tail, and was stretched out as if dead.
Eustace had the impatience of his twenty
years age, and, taking his gun in his hand,
and sticking his tulwar in his belt, he let
himself down by one corner of the scaffolding, and advanced on his prostrate foe. In
another instant the tiger, aroused by the
scent and sight of his enemy, gathered
himself for a final effort, and sprung on
Eustace, striking him backwards, fixing his
teeth in our hero's leg, and tearing his arm
with the paw which was still uninjured.
Kali Khan ran up to fire on the beast, but
withdrew his piece as he saw him drop his
hold on Eustace, and sink back—this time
thoroughly helpless, and, after a shudder

which passed over his massive frame, quite lifeless.

Eustace sat up and tied a handkerchief over his bleeding leg. The natives rushed up to skin the tiger, and possess themselves of the fat, which they cut into strips, put into bottles, and placed in the sun, till, by its heat, the substance was melted down into oil, which, when cool, hardened again into lard.

Eustace obtained the claws for Lyla; and, leaving Kali Khan and the others to skin the tiger, a tedious process, and requiring time to accomplish, without injury to the fur, he proceeded to retrace his steps up the mountain to his tent. The right arm had been wounded by the claws of the wild animal, and some of the small veins having been pierced, the drops " fell heavy one by one, like the first of the thunder shower," as Eustace quoted as he watched them fall.

He had no intention of being poetical, but memory supplied the line involuntarily. He felt in a dreamy state—rather confused in the head, and became conscious that he could not afford to part with any more vital energy. His leg had been bound with his handkerchief, and he had now no choice but to unroll the scarf which was twisted round his red cap, and try with its folds to stop the bleeding.

The beams of the sun had now poured forth their full glory, for the destruction of the tiger had occupied some hours, and Eustace had to rest by the side of a mountain stream to bathe his swimming head and quench his thirst. Probably he remained there longer than he was aware. His leg swelled, and became very painful, and the cool atmosphere of the dashing water was pleasant to him; whilst the pain he felt on movement disposed him to linger. He thought at length that Lyla would be watching for him, and that it would be best for him to reach his tent before he became yet more indisposed for exertion. Very slowly and painfully he climbed the mountain steep, and looked up in the expectation of seeing the figure of Lyla, as usual, framed in the doorway of the tent. But now she was not there.

"No doubt she was inside—not far—she never went far," he said to himself.

Yet he hastened on with a beating heart, which presaged misfortune. He called her by her name, then by every term of endearment. First he called her loudly, but his voice became almost inaudible in the increase of his anxiety. She was nowhere in the tent—he wanted her to bathe his wounds, and pillow his head on her knees.

"Lyla!" he cried, now in a whisper, for his breath and voice were gone—"Lyla!

where are you?" And he stumbled out of the tent, intending to seek for her, he knew not where, and fell on his face insensible.

There he was found by Kali Khan, when this faithful follower returned from the division of the tiger's spoils. He lifted his master into the tent bed, and bathed his face, and washed and rebound his inflamed wounds. Eustace awoke to the consciousness of severe pain in his head, and sickness. Sunstroke had stricken him in his ascent, in addition to his other misfortunes.

"Lyla?" was his first articulate question.

Kali Khan answered, to satisfy his master, with a statement that, feeling lonely, she had gone up to see her mother. This he thought the probable solution of the mystery; and he stated it so decidedly, that Eustace, whose brain was in no condition to discuss probabilities, was content to believe it, and felt a little vexation that she should have left him willingly. He dozed again in the stupor of his pain; and that which surged in his head re-acted on his lacerated limbs.

Kali Khan would have travelled down into the plains to obtain a European doctor, but he dreaded leaving his master. Night came at length, as night comes in the Himalayas, though not in other less-favoured portions of India—cool, dewy, balmy. Though the wounds of Eustace still throbbed, and seemed to burn the surrounding flesh, his head recovered its normal condition, and proved its sanity by tranquil sleep; and Kali Khan, relieved from some of his anxiety, slept also. When Eustace awoke he felt better, but with such pain and stiffness, both in his leg and arm, that he felt he must lie a prisoner for some hours, if not days.

"At any event," he said, "the head's untouched, that 'noble seat of thought'; and

I killed a tiger yesterday—that is a pleasant recollection." And he had his writing materials placed within his reach to give Lady Yorke an account of his adventure. No mention had been made of Lyla to his mother. He respected her too much. He did not find writing very easy; but he forgot the inconvenience of cramped fingers as he went on with the recital. "It is time for you to fetch the milk," he said to Kali Khan; and his attendant, lifting the skin, proceeded to fetch it from the foot of the hill, where the mother of Lyla generally awaited him with it. "Kali! stop! find out why Lyla has not returned."

The Asiatic assented mutely; and so soon as he had departed, Eustace crawled to the door of the tent, with his glass, to watch for Lyla, whom he hoped to see accompany her mother in the descent from her mountain lair. He saw the stream dashing and sparkling down from its coronet of dark pines, throwing a veil of white mist over the rocky ground, but all beside seemed silent and motionless on the neighbouring mountain. He could not even see the accustomed figure of the herds-woman leaving the herd with her skin of milk.

The position in which he had placed himself made his wounded leg more painful by standing on it, and he limped back to his bed. He had no remedy but patience, and in that quality Eustace was not abundant. Few youths of twenty have much of a virtue which, as Fielding sagely observes, is "apt to be worn out with over-exertion," though, in other respects, he was in character more like a man of thirty—circumstances, and the necessity for decision on what course to pursue, and subsequent action on the determination, having made a naturally manly character even more masculine.

Now, however, he was as impatient as a sick child.

"Why did she go?—ungrateful——"

But his sense of justice arrested his vituperations of Lyla in full career.

"She never went willingly," said conscience.

Then Eustace thought of the stripes on her rounded arms and beautiful shoulder, and winced as if his own wounded arm had received the cut of a cane. He must remain quiet if he wished to get well, and regain the possession of his unhappy mistress. He knew how fond of him she was; how she would pine to be restored to him.

He pictured to himself her tears—her cries—her appeals to her mother for pity. And at these thoughts his galloping pulse reminded him that in dwelling on such a picture he was incapacitating himself from rescuing her from her mother's thraldom. A selfish idea suggested itself to his mind. He had so often been puzzled to know what to do with this devoted girl when his leave expired—and but few days now remained to him, unless he could obtain its extension— and now he was relieved of his perplexity. His heart revolted at the thought. He cursed himself for the selfish prudence that had suggested it. He would take Lyla at any risk. He would marry her, and send her to his mother—without the sanctity of such a tie he would not have dared to ask Lady Yorke's protection for the unhappy girl.

And then the juxtaposition even in idea of the untaught savage, however beautiful and devoted, and his refined and cultivated mother, made him bury his burning face in his pillow and groan aloud.

No reflections made him easier. He leaned his head on his left arm to listen, in the hope of hearing her approaching footsteps. Once he felt certain she was coming. He could fancy her rapid displacement of the bushes, and held his breath in anticipation of her approach. A bright-eyed creature of the deer tribe stopped for an instant, and looked at the prostrate youth, through the door of his tent, and then bounded away.

Eustace sank back disappointed. After more than an hour of silence, the flutter of a bird in the branches again awoke his hope, to make him more sad afterwards. It was not till evening that Kali returned. His face bore traces of vexation. He had not brought back Lyla to his master, as he had hoped to do. Not finding the herdswoman at the foot of the mountain, and knowing the anxiety with which news for her would be inquired for by Eustace, he had ascended to her dwelling, to obtain the milk and to ask for her child.

He stated that the woman was sullen, and unwilling to give him any information. She had smiled grimly when he insisted on going into the cave to search for Lyla, of whom he could find no traces. He had offered to purchase the girl on behalf of his master, to obtain her quietly. She laughed, and said,

"The Sahib might have offered that before. Another Sahib had been more generous!" and then she stopped.

Finally she consented that when Kali Khan's master could come to her dwelling he should see Lyla.

" And speak to her ?"

" Yes—if it pleased the Sahib!" and again she laughed.

Kali Khan did not quite understand her, but imagined that, having recovered the girl, she meant to raise her demands for a money compensation for the loss of her daughter's " services ;" barbarism and civilization being agreed on this point.

Reader, if you ever have lost a favourite dog—a creature considered so inferior to his master, but in tenderness, sweetness, and fidelity how superior to his biped companion!—you may remember how the idea of sufferings inflicted on the innocent animal distracted your mind in the uncertainty of its fate.

"What is the name of the Sahib who wished to purchase Lyla?" Eustace inquired.

Kali Khan did not know, but he had picked up in the cave a cover of a letter, which, from the indenting of a small circular mark in the centre, seemed to have been used to wrap up a few pieces of money. The paper was stained and defaced, but it had been originally addressed to —— Saint

Cyr, Esq., care of Messrs. Leckie and Co., Agents, Bombay.

Eustace had heard of this gentleman as travelling about for his pleasure, and report spoke of him as being reckless in the pursuit of women, and cruel in the treatment of them when obtained. He must bid highly to save Lyla, his own Lyla, from such a fate as hers must be, should she be given over to his tender mercies. "The tender mercies of the wicked are cruel!"

Eustace examined carefully the furniture of his tent, to see if there were any marks of a struggle, but he could see none. Could she have accompanied her mother willingly? The clinging embrace with which she had hung on his neck when he last parted from her, had been a sufficient answer to this self-interrogation. There was no help for it; he must wait till he could go himself and see his darling!—how much dearer now in absence than when she had come in the moonlight to his tent, and craved to be his companion!—his love!—his slave!

Two days passed of restless anxiety, but made more tolerable because there was a spot to which hope could point. He should see her—he should speak to her. He would assure her of the tenderness, the fidelity of the love which she, in the plenitude of her passion for him, had always doubted. Hers was so much deeper, so much more intense than his. He loved his mother, he loved his profession, he loved glory. Lyla loved no one but him. She would have died willingly for him. She would have suffered hours of agony to save him a moment's pain, or even vexation.

All this should be made up to her when she returned to him. He thought how wistfully her eyes used to follow him when he went out to hunt. How she had used to crave permission to follow him, and how sternly she had been rebuked for the proposition. Her pleading eyes, as he had seen them when he was about to attack the tiger, haunted him. What an expression of mute suffering there had been in those helpless looks. They came back to him now—now that it was too late to answer their appeal. In the hurry of that busy expedition these supplications had been unheeded. Years after those yearning eyes pursued Eustace, waking and sleeping, and burnt their memory into his troubled brain.

It was before sunrise that Eustace at length started on his journey to the mountain cavern. For two hours Kali Khan had previously been engaged in pouring tepid water over the wounds in his leg, to diminish their inflammation. The expedition must be both tedious and painful to Eustace, for his arms were nearly as much in requisition as his legs, so much ground had to be got over in climbing. His left arm had never regained its deficiency of bone, and was consequently less strong than the right arm usually; but now the latter was stiff and painful, and could not support much of his weight.

Kali put forward a claim to aid his master in the ascent, and Eustace consented to accept his attendance, stipulating only that he should remain at a distance and out of earshot of his conversation with the herdswoman.

No extension of leave had arrived, and Eustace felt that he must return to the plains on the day following his expedition to the mountains. His hope was that, by paying a handsome sum to the mother, he might recover Lyla, and make her the companion of his journey. He had in his pocket the tiger's claws, which he hoped would make his darling's eyes sparkle with joy. He had also provided gold—more than he liked to think of—to buy her back.

His step became more elastic and hopeful as he reached the side of the cascade. By going higher up the stream he crossed easily, by the aid of the fallen fir, to where he saw the flutter of the ends of a shawl, which bound the waist of Lyla's mother. She was motionless, for the wind disturbed only her drapery. Her stony face seemed cut out like that of a sullen Sphinx against the blue sky at her back.

Kali remained quietly awaiting his master's return, and watched his approach to the herdswoman. She rose as Eustace approached, and salaamed profoundly, with a sinister smile on her face; which Kali knew, and trembled for some misfortune impending over his master. They then moved away and were lost to view. There was silence for about a quarter of an hour, and Kali caught sight of the two figures descending the sides of the cataract. Then again a silence—they had stopped. Kali heard a cry or groan from his master, and a peal of mocking laughter from the woman, which was caught up and repeated by all the echoes, till it seemed a chorus dying away in the distance. Kali rushed across the chasm and bounded over the space that divided him from his master, who was stretched on the soft turf, pale and insensible.

The woman had left him, and was swinging her gigantic frame up the acclivity, and was soon lost in the distance. Kali stooped over his master to see if he had suffered any injury. In doing this he looked involuntarily beyond him, as he lay on the edge of the deep, still water which made a great basin by the side of the dashing cataract.

It was very clear—it revealed the white pebbles shining in its depths—it revealed also a human form reposing in its cold bed. The arms were tied behind her, too tightly for extrication, the long dark hair and the fringe of the scarf Eustace had given her moved slightly with the ripple of the water. The horror of her face was hidden; and from that trivial movement it seemed as if life still lingered. When Eustace recovered the shock which had deprived him of sense, he rushed to the edge of the rock, and, deceived by the ripple, would have plunged in to rescue her. Kali's wiry arms withheld him from that madness.

"Stop, Sahib," he said, and taking a fragment of rock, he flung it in, and thereby displaced the body; and Eustace saw—and hid his face, and shouted and yelled in his rage and despair!

CHAPTER II.

"When vain dreams are stirr'd with sighing near the morning,
To my own her phantom lips I feel approach;
And her smile at eve breathes o'er me without warning
From its speechless, pale, perpetual reproach.

When life's dawning glimmer yet had all the tint there
Of the orient, in the freshness of the grass,
(Ah! what feet since then have trodden out the print there),
Did her soft and silent footsteps fall and pass."

OWEN MEREDITH.

EUSTACE hastened his departure from the Himalayas—he could not remain in the neighbourhood of a horror so great—of a sorrow so absorbing. In the few days which followed, his mind seemed to reel under the shock he had received, in seeing the corpse of her on whom he had hoped to lavish the treasures of his love—the intensity of his tenderness. He had felt in their separation how much she had outbid him in her devotion. He had meant to pay it back, and make her future life happy, even at the sacrifice of his own comfort.

Let no one lay " the flattering unction to his soul" that the future may rectify the faults of the present. Eustace's memory conjured up instance after instance when he had been irritated by the expressions of her love, and had taken no care to conceal it. A man kicks aside the little spaniel who fawns on him, if he has a letter which worries him, or if the post brings not one which he has expected, or if he is too hot, or too cold, or wears a tight boot, or has a toothache or headache. Men treat women in the same manner—*if they dare*—that is, if the wife brought no grist to the domestic mill; or if she was taken from a lower grade; if she has no relations to take her part; and, mostly, if she is meek-spirited—the worst quality she can possess. That "ornament of a meek and quiet spirit" will not do in the present day, though it might have done in the time of the Apostles.

Look into the cottages, and you will find the best kept and the best conducted are those in which the woman is said to have "a fine spirit of her own." The cabin of the meek-spirited woman is generally dirty and neglected, for the husband prefers the alehouse from which the female eloquence affrights him—the meek wife loses heart, and throws up the game.

It seems a principle in human nature to domineer when it can. There is one throned high on the domestic dunghill, amongst all the inhabitants of the farm-yard; one who crows loudest, and whose voice strikes terror into the feathered breasts of all his companions.

Mastership is disputed between dogs, to the death.

If one human creature is strong, and the other weak, the strong will almost unconsciously rule with an iron rod, especially if love makes the subjection greater on the part of the oppressed.

With such a companion, Eustace might have degenerated into a selfish tyrant. With every wish anticipated, every ruffle of ill-temper tenderly smoothed over, he was on the high road towards becoming truly an Anglo-Indian. Lyla, the fragrant wild flower which he had crushed unwittingly in his path, by the horror of her death awakened such remorseful memories as made him, in his future intercourse with those dependent on him, slow to anger and of great pity.

The circumstances which led to this catastrophe he learnt before he left the neighbourhood. The cowkeeper had ascended to the hut, and found Lyla where she had remained at the door of the tent, watching for Eustace, and speculating, by the flight of the unclean birds, in what place the contest was going on with the tiger. She feared her mother too much to refuse to accompany her home, and probably comforted herself with the reflection that as in their primitive dwelling there were no doors, and, consequently, no bolts and bars, she might easily return to Eustace when her mother slept.

Her mother had been of this opinion also, and had arranged accordingly with Mr. Saint Cyr to be ready with his servant to take possession of Lyla, and carry her off as soon as she reached her mother's cave. They had crossed the cataract by aid of the fallen tree, but before they turned the corner into the recess, the mother took from Lyla the scarf which Eustace had given her, and tied her arms behind her, that she might make no resistance to her captors. An instant after Lyla perceived what her fate would be, if she succumbed to it. She knew how small was her chance of escape, but death would be preferable to life without Eustace, and in the enforced embraces of another. She darted away, helpless from her imprisoned arms. She knew that in swiftness of foot none of the four people bent on restraining her flight could equal her. She would go to Eustace—to where she had seen the vultures directing their flight— what mattered it if the tiger seized and devoured her? Eustace would know she was true to him. Away she goes, panting and breathless with terror and excitement. She reaches the tree which spans the cataract, and steps on it. Involuntarily her movements are more slow and careful. Her pursuers have thus time to come up with her. Saint Cyr's foot is on the trunk of the tree, his hand has seized the end of the scarf, she darts forward, staggers, and falls, unable without the aid of her arms to balance herself as she was wont. For an instant she struggles on one of the projecting fragments of cliff over which the water is dashing. She strives vainly to release her arms, bound with such cruel strength and compactness. The scarf had been jerked from the hands of Saint Cyr as she fell. "Save her! save!" he cries, but the native servants care not to endanger their lives. As they hesitate the stream rolls her over and over helplessly. Blood mingles with and tints the dashing water, and Lyla lies dead in the great depth at the bottom of the cascade.

Eustace was glad—or rather was satisfied to be in the sphere of his duties again—when he rejoined his regiment at Sindhora.

He had come at evening a considerable distance, and was depressed in mind, and weary in body, but work was to be done, and his spirits rose at the prospect. A spy was waiting to see him—one of many men whom Eustace, who combined the character of Ulysses with that of Achilles, kept in his employment by the expenditure of funds of his own.

From this man he learnt that a band of rebels had been in his absence infesting the neighbourhood, and that a native magistrate of considerable importance, who had incurred their enmity by giving information respecting them to the British authorities, had been carried off by them to the jungle, where, on the following morning, they meant to hang him. They would have done this at once, but waited to know whether Tantia Topee would examine him first, and were every hour expecting an answer from that rebel chief. To pursue these men, and retake their captive, was the intention of Eustace, who selected Kali Khan and eleven others to accompany him. The guide was to direct them to the secluded spot in the jungle where the Budmaches were encamped.

After proceeding about twelve miles the fitful flicker of lights in the forest showed where the enemy were hidden. No horses could penetrate these woods, so Eustace left three of his party to hold them, and proceeded on foot. This was not an easy undertaking, for the darkness of the night seemed solid, excepting in the distant occasional sparkle of the camp fires of the Budmaches, which rose and fell at intervals. The expedition proceeded slowly, feeling rather than perceiving their way. They did this for three miles, and suddenly found themselves within twenty-six feet of the enemy. Eustace had heard they were but twenty in number, but peering cautiously through the thicket, he was astonished at the frequency of the fires, and the number of men encamped around them. By a rough calculation he thought they could not be less than eighty or ninety men. Some of them were sleeping, some eating, some keeping watch over the unhappy prisoner and his brother, who were seated, with bound arms and dejected countenances, under a tree, and a little withdrawn from the circle of their guards.

"If I fail," thought the young man, "I shall be called a reckless fool, who had no business to endanger the lives of his men by his rashness, though he might have done as he pleased with his own. If I do not try to rescue these prisoners, an opportunity will have been neglected, and I shall be wretched to the end of my life."

He and his men fired a volley, and Eustace, Kali Khan, and one more rushed in, attacking the Sepoys with their swords. The panic was universal. They wounded nine or ten men, who rolled themselves away into the shadows. The rest fled, leaving the prisoners, whose bonds were cut, but who were too much stupefied to be of any use in their own defence. A rebel in a red coat attracted the attention of our hero, who ran on to attack him; but the Sepoy turned to the right, and fell in with Kali Khan, who closed with him, and they rolled together into a nullah, and disappeared in the darkness.

Uneasy for his favourite servant, Eustace jumped in after them, in time to see Kali Khan, by the fleeting light, busily employed in cutting off the head of his antagonist, in a manner which rejoiced the heart of his master.

"Was there no pity—no relenting ruth?"

No—there is neither when a man's spirit is up, and he sees blood flowing like water. He feels elated at the risk—conscious of a nobleness in his disdain of peril—triumphant in anticipated success. Now, however, a change came over Eustace. His men, saving two, had not followed him. It seemed absurd that three men should have routed eighty-five, but this was the fact—

"So much confusion magnified the foe."

The rest of his men had stood outside, and yelled like demons, a proceeding which was very effective in increasing the idea of their numbers.

When Kali Khan emerged from his ditch, hot and breathless with his exertions, he found the third man, maddened by the sight of the blood he had shed, incapable of self-guidance, and led him back to those who had remained on the edge of the nullah.

Eustace saw that retreat was imperative, if he was to get his men back safely. The Sepoys might return so soon as they found they were not pursued. The ground was so broken that he and his followers had fallen more than once,—sometimes from the inequalities of the surface, sometimes over the bodies of dead or wounded men.

When he regained the outside of the encampment, he found that the spy who had conducted them had fallen down insensible, from an over-dose of opium, taken on the principle on which doubtful horsemen, on a hunting morning, apply to their flasks at the sight of an ugly fence. To leave him extended on the ground would be to leave him to death—perhaps to torture. The men, therefore, had to lead the mad soldier by his cummerbund, and to take it by turns to carry the heavy body of the spy. Eustace, bringing up the rear, followed the *cortége* with an anxious heart and a watchful ear. Nervousness had now succeeded to ardour. The thought of being surrounded and cut off in the thick jungle made him fret and chafe at the slow pace at which they were obliged to proceed; but the terror that his night attack had carried to the breasts of the mutineers was too potent to allow them to rally immediately.

The three miles were at length accomplished; and once mounted, Eustace felt himself again, and ready to encounter any danger which might befall him; but none threatened, and falling asleep that night he saw between his heavy eyelids the forms of the two rescued men, to whom he had extended the hospitality of his small domain, and who, too much excited to sleep, spoke in half-articulate words of wonder and thankfulness to each other—of wonder as to the sphere from which Eustace had descended, or ascended; and of thankfulness to the angel, or devil, who had saved their lives.

Eustace slept, and for the first time saw in his dreams other images than that of the cascade in the Himalaya; but the shock received by his nervous system could not soon be rectified. The wounds inflicted by the tiger, too, never thoroughly healed, threatened fresh inflammation, and Eustace, sick in mind and in body, threw up his command and returned to England. His indifferent health made him moody, and threatened to make him morose, so much are the best compacted creatures of clay subject to ills that flesh is heir to. His wounds refused to heal till he had been for a week at sea; but his spirits did not for months recover the loss of the young Asiatic.

CHAPTER III.

> "My son! my son!
> After this length of time, this tedious absence,
> Do I behold thy face? Ah! fold thine arms
> Around me—clasp me to thy bosom—lean
> Thy cheek against my fond cheek—shade my breast
> With the dark ringlets of thy clust'ring hair.
> Can I believe I hold thee in my arms,
> Unlooked for thus, so much beyond my hopes?
> What shall I say to thee?—how tell thee all?
> To touch thee thus, to hear thy voice is joy,
> Is transport; and my throbbing heart once more
> Feels its old raptures. O my son! my son!
> Long hast thou left thy father's house forsaken."
> *Translation from Euripides.*

THREE years had passed when Eustace returned to his mother, again invalided—three years which seemed to have acted as ten on his character, constitution, and appearance. "Sir Eustace is come!" resounded through the quiet household; and Myra rushed to the drawing-room, where stood, leaning on the chimney-piece, a grave, thoughtful, bearded man in a fez, enveloped in a military cloak. She flung herself towards him with a cry of eager joy, that was almost a scream. He met her quietly, with his hand outstretched, and with a kiss on her forehead, so deliberate, that it seemed as if he were looking for a place where care had not left a wrinkle. But no coldness could damp Myra's joy, or diminish her pride in her son. True, he was bronzed—worse than that, he was yellow and ill; but he *must* recover now—now he *must* stay with her. No wonder he looked ill—three years under canvas, exposed to scorching sun and drenching rain, would make the healthiest suffer. But he had won honours and credit beyond any that ever she could have dreamt of; and the ugly cross, so coveted above its beautiful rival of France, or, rather, the bit of ribbon which indicated its possession, was fastened to his faded uniform, in juxtaposition with that of the Legion of Honour. Myra had "an over-payment of delight."

"Better a thousand times than being senior wrangler, which I had so coveted for you," she said proudly.

He smiled sadly. Honours, like other things, seem less valuable when they are grasped. Rosamund's purple jar carries its moral through life.

"I am come to be nursed, mother," he said; "you are never tired of nursing me, I know. And now let us have some tea and dry toast. I am like the young man in the old Scotch ballad, 'weary with hunting, and fain would lie down,' and shall be glad to go to bed early."

"Will you go at once, and let me sit by

your bed-side?—do let me?—shall I send for the doctor?"

"No, dear mother, we will have our tea here, and you shall play me the old 'Zouave March,' which, in my hunting Tantia Topee, I have nearly forgotten. Talking of hunting, do the hounds meet near here next week? A gallop will do me good."

After tea he revived, and challenged Myra to their old amusement, chess. He had not played since he had done so on the voyage out to India, going round the Cape, but he played better now than before. His intellect was strengthened, and Myra's maternal feelings were gratified even in the defeat she underwent from his superior skill. Formerly their play had been equal.

She stole into his bed-room before he was awake on the following morning, as if to be assured that her happiness had not been a dream. It was with a feeling akin to awe that she looked on that worn, yellow face.

> "All it had felt, inflicted, passed and proved,
> Hushed into depths beyond the watcher's diving."

Could that firmly-cut countenance, handsome, but harsh in its lines, have been once the baby the circling outlines of whom she had nourished on her bosom? It seemed strange that so few years should have made an alteration so striking. As she stood by his side he uttered some sharp, quick words in a barbarous tongue, as if giving an order. Myra started, and the slight sound made by the rustle of her silk dress awoke the sleeper, who sprang up and seized his revolver, with flashing, suspicious eyes—then, falling back, exclaimed, with a faint laugh,

"Ah! mother, how you startled me!"

Eustace was as nervous as ever, seemingly. In the course of the day Myra found her boy was not the same as he who had left her three years before. He had been away from her influence, and showed it. No one could have written more dutifully, every fortnight, nor inconvenienced himself more than Eustace had done, that she might receive letters by every Indian post; but they were necessarily brief, and recorded facts, not opinions.

"Do not think me neglectful that my letters are not longer. Shall I tell you how I am writing now? Fancy yourself, in the dusk of the evening, on the borders of a lake like that in our own park. The wind is high, and with trouble you take a sheet of thin letter-paper from your valise, and sitting on the bank, try to steady it on your knees—nothing flat on which to place it—fresh puffs of wind flutter the paper every moment. As I write the quick eye of my native servant has detected something more than trunks of trees in a cluster of them further down on the borders of the lake. In an instant the letter is thrust away, and mounting the still saddled horses, we spur them into the water, across to the dark mass that loomed so suspiciously. We are received with a volley, and then see hostile troopers dispersing over the plain singly, with the conviction that in the broken ground their capture or destruction one by one will not reward the pursuers. How many letters would you or any one write under these circumstances? Yet, if it be not written, and sent forty miles to the post, my mother will not have the comfort of one on her breakfast-table on the morning when the arrival of the packet telegraphed from Marseilles has led her to expect it. So, mother mine, excuse shortcomings!"

And his mother thought both the letters and the writer as perfect as possible.

One day, soon after his return, however,

she saw a shabby Letts' Diary of the past year on his table.

"Your diary!—oh! Eustace, how interesting it must be!—may I read it?"

"No, mother," he replied, quietly and decidedly.

Myra's face flushed, as if she had received a blow on those faded cheeks. She had a confused feeling that she ought not to have asked—that a door had been metaphorically slammed in her face—that she was ill-used, because she felt that every word she wrote or had ever written might be read by Eustace, and his heart was shut up from hers. She went out softly, and walking to the hot-house, selected the finest bunch of Muscat grapes, which Eustace had preferred in former days, and brought them to his room, where he had been taking his breakfast in dressing-gown and slippers, reading intently Napier's "Peninsular War." She put the berries near him silently, and he stretched out his hand abstractedly, and ate them without seeming conscious that his mother had brought them as a small peace-offering for having asked what he had not chosen to grant.

Utterly unconscious of having inflicted any uneasiness, and with a vague sensation that he was gratifying his mother for something agreeable, he scarcely knew what, he read and ate till the last grape was abstracted from the stem; and having felt about without looking for more, and not finding them, he continued to read whilst she sat near, seemingly reading, but really only holding the book as an excuse for an occupation, whilst she looked up at her son with loving eyes.

"When will the county paper arrive?" said Eustace.

"I will order it to be sent," replied his

mother. "I should have thought of it, but I take the *Times*."

"Ah! yes; but do write for the —— *Chronicle*—I want to see the meets."

The next day Eustace's native Syce had contrived to explain to the servants that his master wanted to buy horses, and the intelligence brought dealers from far and near. Very picturesque did this tall, wiry native look in his snowy linen, dark skin, and gleaming eyes. Eustace had selected him for his courage and determination. In one of his campaigns he had been roused from the deep sleep which had succeeded his capture of a rebel chief, by a frightful confusion of noises. Eight or nine stallions had broken from their fastenings, and were knotted together in a fearful struggle, neighing, stamping, biting, and kicking each other with as much ferocity as if they had been human enemies.

Before Eustace could reach the scene of confusion, he saw in the clear moonlight a tall dark youth spring on the most powerful of the rearing animals, and stretching his lean arms out, crook his fingers in the horse's mouth, and pull, till he turned him out of the affray. When he had given him to another native to hold, he returned to the still heaving and rebellious multitude, and disposed of another and another in the same manner, till some sharp lashes from a whip disposed of the less vicious.

The perceptions of Eustace, become almost Anglo-Indian in custom, made him turn with loathing from the sight of an English groom dressing a horse in nether garments never intended for washing, and in a shirt which had been put on clean a week previously.

"We manage those things better in

India," he thought, as he turned with complacency to look at Kali Khan in his faultless linen, daily washed. Both master and servant recognised the points of a good horse, and Eustace soon was the possessor of three very handsome and good goers, but decidedly with wills of their own.

For this Eustace cared not, but his mother cared a great deal. The poor lady went out to look at the hunters when Eustace tried them, and stood with a white face and cold lips whilst the horse kicked all the way from the stables to the end of a long avenue.

"Do let Kali Khan fetch your *jacket*," said the poor mother in a tremulous shriek, to reach him through the vista of trees.

"Nonsense, mother. I'm not going to hunt in a jacket. The horse must be taught to bear the skirts of my coat," he said, partly turning his head, in words which were jerked out by the involuntary impetus given to them by the horse's hind legs. At length he came back, and flung the reins to his servant, and offered his arm to his mother. He had ridden "Sultan" at a gate, at which period Lady Yorke had compressed her eyelids and lips, that she might neither see nor scream. A shout of satisfaction from the coachman and groom made her open her eyes, to see that Eustace had returned safely over the gate.

"You will not buy that dreadful creature?"

"Mother, would you make me a milksop? Do you know I shall get that horse thirty pounds cheaper than I otherwise must have paid, on account of this little trick of his; and really 'tis the best possible movement to set my liver all right again."

"Do you mean to keep the horse for the term of his natural life? Does it not strike you that if you wish to sell him, you may not get a customer with a convenient liver complaint, nor one willing to adopt that unusual mode of cure?"

"Never mind," he said, smiling sweetly, and his mother thought how beautifully shaped was the short upper lip, shaded by a moustache—"I am not frequently nervous now. I have sometimes felt the bitterness of death—in its anticipation very bitter; but it seems to me that inevitable tyrant cannot reach me, when I am so near you, and on my own land. Now I will tell you when I felt most nervous. 'I want to make your flesh creep,' as the fat boy says in Pickwick. It was in our pursuit of Tantia Topee—my chief was ill, and the management of the chase after the rebel was virtually in my hands. This made me more eager to proceed, though I was a good deal exhausted by days of continued riding, relieved by nights of two hours duration only. My spies had returned with no reliable intelligence, and instead of lying down after a forced march, I took a trooper's horse, who had only been ridden twenty miles instead of forty, as mine had been, and went out myself to see if I could track the fugitives. I took one man with me, and rode in the direction which previous information had pointed out as likely to lead to the accomplishment of my object; and reaching the mouth of a gorge between two hills, I distinctly could trace the marks of the camels' hoofs on the soft sand. Tantia had camels—we had none—and this decided the fact of his having passed through the ravine. I sent my companion back with the intelligence, and an order that the troops should follow me.

" A small village was situated on one side of the steep, and I shouted to the inhabitants to bring me some chupatties and milk. After a pause of indecision, an old man brought me some, and after drinking the milk, I was so exhausted that I dismounted, and lay down in the shade and fell asleep, meaning to wait there for my troops."

"I hope you paid for the milk?" said Lady Yorke.

He pressed her arm tenderly.

"Yes, my dear mother. I learnt from you to be 'true and just in all my dealings.' I must say, however, that my countrymen probably had not had mothers so conscientious, for few did so."

"Go on."

"I don't know how long I slept, for I was very weary; but a slight noise in the distance awakened me, and I saw at the mouth of the gorge an armed native riding towards me, whom I took for one of my own men. I mounted, and rode to meet him, to receive intelligence from my chief, when I saw that he was a rebel, by his preparing to shoot me. This was unpleasant, but not the worst—he was followed by several others, fully armed, and well mounted. The villagers swarmed down the sides of the steep to join in the chase of the hunted Englishman, and I found I was caught in a trap, and had little chance of escape.

"The defile between the hills rose almost precipitously, and having been formed by a mountain torrent, it was filled with fragments of rocks and large stones, difficult to surmount at one's leisure, and with a good horse; but almost impossible with an exhausted one, and a crowd of bloodthirsty ruffians behind one. I spurred the poor beast on, expecting him to drop at every fresh obstacle to be surmounted. My breath grew shorter, and my heart beat almost to suffocation. I had *met* death frequently, but never before *fled* from it; and no one who has not tried can tell how much easier is the former than the latter. I strove as one in a dream to get over the fearful obstacles to my progress, and every now and then the shouts of my pursuers grew nearer and nearer.

"I was nearly at the top of the defile. I could see what I believed to be the rebel troops passing in lines over the green turf which clothed the open ground on the heights.

"'No chance of escape there,' I thought; yet it seemed hard to die, and never see you again, mother. When one troop had passed, there was a space before another followed. I will ride between them. I thought at least those brutes behind me shall not have the pleasure of killing me; so I·darted over the last grey fragment of stone, and got my horse on the turf.

"I looked for an instant with dazzled eyes, and was hailed by my own men, whom I had taken for rebels. My messenger had not appeared, and my chief had pushed on from other news he had received.

"After living amongst such scenes, my mother, you will not grudge my buying a kicking horse."

Lady Yorke could be silent; but, doting on her son with a fondness which made the passion of her life, she found that the vague fears which had possessed her in his absence had been less difficult to bear than the daily anxieties that marked his return. He hunted, and rode foremost at any risk. She knew that he would, and always feared an accident. When the days grew shorter, she used to sit at the window and listen for the click of the latch of the park gate, or the more distant sounds of the barking of dogs at the farmers' in the neighbourhood which he might pass, when the rain descended, and the sky was black as ink, distracted by the thought that it was impossible to tell by what road he might return—by the idea that he might be at that moment, when she was surrounded by every comfort and luxury, lying crushed and helpless under his horse, and might lie there for hours before the tardy morning light would bring observation, and, with observation, aid.

Then she would calculate at what hour darkness must have ended the chase, and how long it would take to ride home a tired horse over a given number of miles. "That brute, too, Sultan!" But she was half-consoled to think how perfect he was at timber. She who had hated all sports was "well up" now in all the meets, and their various distances. She knew which way the fox was likely to take in a certain wind, and the position of every cover in the neighbourhood. The nights were not always pitch dark, nor the meets so very distant; and even when they were so, what joy it was to greet the wearied rider as he dismounted, to see his bespattered horse led off to the stable, and to bring his master to his closely curtained bed-room and blazing fire, to look back fondly as he became indistinctly seen through the steam of his bath, drawing off his saturated boots; and then to wait patiently, though dinner had been kept back —*i.e.*, spoiled—for an hour and a half, till he emerged, " with liquid odours crowned," and full dressed, to conduct her to the dining-room; and then to finish the evening with a game of chess.

Eustace had enlisted in his cause the services of a fashionable tailor, and had found, with better reason than the original speaker, "himself to be a marvellous proper man." His mother admired him more in the faded scarlet fez, with a purple tassel, and the tattered green tunic of the Irregular Horse, than in the faultless turn-out of Mr. Hill of Bond Street. But young gentlemen do not, as a rule, dress to please their mothers, as Lady Yorke soon discovered.

"Mother, I shall not return here this evening after hunting. It is a long distance to Earlscliff, and I shall dine and sleep at Sir Richard Levinge's."

"Oh! my dear!" said his mother.

"Well?" inquired Eustace, and there was the slightest suspicion of impatience and defiance in his tone.

"Nothing," said his mother, sadly; "only I shall not know whether you are home safe at night."

"Yes, you shall, my dear mother," he

said, smiling tenderly. "Kali Khan shall wait there till I return, and ride back my hack horse—so you shall have the earliest intelligence of my broken neck. I will not even detain him to see Sultan properly cleaned and bedded down, but trust Sir Richard's groom for that. There, now, that is a sacrifice a woman cannot appreciate!"

"Yes, I do appreciate it, my son, and am very grateful for it."

Lady Yorke, in the deep and continued grief of her widowhood, had declined society, and society had soon reconciled itself to her absence, as that social power always does. What had begun in depression, had been continued in shyness on the part of her ladyship. Her neighbours did not care for her dead husband, beyond the exclamation of "what a pity!" as the manner of his death became known. They cared less for his little son, and therefore she shut herself up in her own domains, not having any community of interest with her neighbours, and gave all her time and thoughts to the improvement of Eustace's estate.

"He shall find a fine unencumbered income when he returns," she said. She had not spared her handsome jointure for this good work; she would have given every penny she possessed to have purchased any advantages or pleasure for him. But she forgot that there were pleasures and advantages that money thus lavished could not purchase, and that she had only her own society, which was insufficient to his happiness; whilst his presence was to her a never-failing spring of delight.

Thus, whilst Eustace was thrown amongst his compeers in the field, he felt disposed to accept some of the numerous invitations to dine and sleep at the various country houses in the neighbourhood.

"Lady Yorke is an invalid, and never leaves home, I believe," was constantly said to him by some hostess, who was not sorry to have the young heir unwatched by a clever, lynx-eyed mother.

"My mother's health is perfect," her son would reply; "but she has never found society necessary to her happiness, and does not, therefore, care to mix in it."

I am not sure that the poor lady did not regret her exclusiveness when the carriage drove round to take Eustace to some gay scene which she was not invited to share. Then, when the choice hot-house flower was fastened in his button-hole, and the slight kiss received on her brow, she sat alone as the dim twilight gathered round, looking over the still landscape till it faded into night, and pictured to herself the lighted table, the damask curtains, the vessels of gold and silver, the merry laugh, and the pleased attention to Eustace, paid by some fair girl at his side, who would usurp *her* place in his heart. Then she would clasp her slender hands on her knees, and feel withered by jealous fears. Of course they would all try to catch him—the golden treasures she had so sedulously accumulated for her darling would only make him more desirable. They, however, had been needless. Young, handsome, well-born, valiant, and titled, he had been all wealthy enough to have been considered "a catch" without her care.

To Eustace the charm of woman's society came like the dawning of a new scene. His Crimean campaign had been followed by a slow recovery from his wound and subsequent fever. Then, in his three years under canvas in India, he had seen only native women, unadorned by the charms of refinement and civilization. No wonder he thought the elegant and cultivated ladies whom he met at Earlscliff, many of whom were young and lovely, as but "a little lower than the angels;" no wonder that every dinner-party produced some morning engagement on the following day. Another and another still succeeded, for other country families were anxious to entertain so gallant and agreeable a guest; and Lady Yorke began to fade faster, and grow thinner every day, till Eustace was at length stricken with some compunction at not having sooner perceived her unhappiness.

"My mother has always lived alone since my father's death," he said, mentally. "Why should she pine for company now?"

Alas! no thought can help us to the feelings of those further advanced in life than ourselves. Experience comes uselessly to show us what we inflicted unknowingly, when we can never recall what we have made others suffer. Lady Yorke was too fond of Eustace to accept the society he wished to bestow elsewhere, but it is not in the heart of a man to understand what she suffered in his absence. Her whole life had been one long dream of him. He might now have repaid her devotion; but he did not understand that she pined for his company—was childishly anxious when he was out late at nights, and used to sit up in bed listening, leaning on her elbow frequently till the night light paled before the first saffron streak of day, before she heard the wheels of his dog-cart crunching the gravel, and knew that he had arrived safely.

It would have been better to have sat up; but Eustace, finding her in the drawing-room, on several occasions, on his return from dinner-parties, had extorted a promise that she should go to bed. He did not suspect how sleepless that bed was to her. Sometimes she led him to speak of the different ladies he had met, and tried to gather which he most admired when he spoke of their beauty, their wit, their cultivation, their refinement.

Lady Yorke, with great feminine tact, discovered how much of what appeared to her son to be pure gold, was but tinsel. She knew her own sex far better than the truthful, noble character sitting beside her, who, incapable of moving in any but a direct path to his object, could not believe that the fair creatures who made life seem to him a beautiful dream, had anything circuitous in their line of conduct. She was not herself an adept in concealing her feelings, and Eustace was quick in perceiving that she did not share his enthusiasm as to the ladies he was in the habit of meeting, and became silent on the subject. This made his mother more unhappy, as she believed there was something to be concealed.

CHAPTER IV.

"Oh, do not hold it for a crime,
In the bold hero of my rhyme,
For stoic look
And meet rebuke,
He lacked the heart or time;
As round the band of syrens trip,
He kissed one damsel's laughing lip,
And pressed another's proffered hand—
Spoke to them all in accents bland."

SCOTT.

IT was lucky for Eustace that so many fair creatures strove to win him. Had he been placed for a week in a country house with one only, and no chaperon, his fate had been sealed; but whilst the hazel eyes of one sweet girl—eyes of a rich velvety brown, like the back of a humble bee—

beamed on him softly from black lashes on his right, the bright liquid blue of those on his left, dancing with mirth and *espièglerie*, shot right to his heart, till the queenly, voluptuous, full-blown beauty of the widow opposite and her conversation—so seemingly natural, and really studied—made the young man hesitate as to which deserved the palm of attractiveness.

Lady Yorke was a fine performer on the piano; and Eustace, who had a delicate ear for music, but knew nothing of the notes, would delight to sit and read for hours during the day, when not tempted away by pressing engagements, whilst listening to her fine perfect execution of the Sonatas of Beethoven, or the Masses of Mozart.

"Do the ladies play at Earlscliff?" she said one day.

"Yes, most of them. One girl plays everything at sight—you cannot put before her any piece, however difficult, but she will play it at sight."

"She must indeed play wonderfully!" said Lady Yorke drily. "Give her this Sonata of Beethoven's, and see if she plays it at sight."

Eustace took it gladly, pleased that his mother took any interest in his associates. When he next returned home, Lady Yorke asked, with seeming indifference, did Miss Danvers play the Sonata.

"Oh! yes."

"I cannot think she played it at sight!"

"Oh! yes," said Eustace; "I stood at the back of her chair and turned the leaves."

Lady Yorke was sceptical; she let the matter drop for a few days, and when she saw Eustace deep in the "Twelve Decisive Battles," she began and played through the Sonata—the first part containing the Swiss cattle call, the imitation of the nightingale, and the conclusion of the storm.

"Oh! mother, how exquisite—how charming! I never heard that before."

"I daresay not, my dear," said his mother quietly; and she knew he had been imposed on by Miss Danvers' having played some old school music by rote, trusting to his ignorance of the characters of music not to be betrayed. She was too politic to prove that she was in the right. No man is gratified for being warned or undeceived. Tell a passing stranger that his pocket-handkerchief hangs out too temptingly for the pick-pockets, and he will feel inclined to d—n your eyes for your interference.

"These are the kind of women out of which he will select one to be my companion for the remainder of my life," she thought sadly. "I wish I could see them, and try to influence his choice."

Vain wish!—every man likes in such

matters to select for himself. Lady Yorke had hoped that when the London season commenced, and the county families flocked to Town, she should have more of her son's company; but he expressed a wish to go thither also, and she was too much flattered by the point he made, that she should accompany him, to resist his little speech.

"I cannot be happy without you to welcome me to my home, wherever that may be, mother."

"You will be choosing some one else to welcome your returning home soon, Eustace, I dare say. I ought not to complain if it makes you happy."

"Mother, I will never commit myself till you have seen and pronounced on the woman I wish to make my wife. If you do not think her worthy to be your daughter-in-law, she shall not be Lady Eustace Yorke."

"Oh! Eustace, what a promise!—can you keep it?"

"When did I ever break my word, mother?"

"Never," said Lady Yorke, looking at him with eyes brimming with tenderness.

"Then 'tis a bargain," he said gaily, for the sight of his mother's tears always shocked him. She was not given to weeping.

It was shortly after this that Eustace told his mother that he was in love—perhaps not yet *in* love, but much attracted. Lady Yorke could hardly repress a shiver at the intelligence, which increased, evidently, at the information given by Eustace as to the belongings of his charmer.

"You see, my mother," he continued, "I have seen her but twice, and I dare say I shall forget her again, if such an effort be necessary, especially when cub-hunting begins, which is better than nothing. In the meantime, I should like to marry Miss Rivers, unless there should be in your mind any just cause or impediment to that result. I trust to your honour to give her a fair judgment."

"Yes," said Lady Yorke, slowly; "but, Eustace, I really think a soldier should have nothing to do with social ties. There is something so fine in the ancient order of Knights Hospitallers, Knights of Malta, Knights of St. John! Ambition made the object of their lives; then every energy of mind and body was given to increase the prosperity of their order; they were soldiers, and nothing more—but what grand soldiers!"

Eustace stood up to his full height, and turned his head to the distant landscape, whilst his blue eyes flashed with conscious pride as he repeated the beautiful lines of Tennyson—

> "Thy voice is heard 'midst rolling drums,
>   Which beat to battle as he stands—
> Thy face upon his fancy comes,
>   And gives the battle to his hands.
>
> "One moment, as the trumpets blow,
>   He sees thy brood about thy knee—
> The next like fire he meets the foe,
>   And strikes him dead for thine and thee."

"Yes, very exquisite poetry; but is it true in fact? Do you think that you would be as willing to lead a forlorn hope if you fancied to yourself your young wife with her brood about her knee?"

"I don't know," said Eustace, thoughtfully. "I do not much imagine I should think of my wife and children under such circumstances. War has its own claims and duties. The rolling drum does not bring with it thoughts of firesides or homesteads. Unless, indeed, the soldier is so unfortunate that the tide of devastation floods his own land, and then indeed he may 'meet the foe, and strike him dead,' for the protection of his Lares and Penates."

"Then, if you think of your wife and children, you will not be so good, or, more correctly, so impetuous a soldier. If you do not think of them, you will be an indifferent husband and father. Now, should you marry, under the circumstances?"

"Mother! mother! do not urge me! Whilst *you* are almost an angel, *I* am but a mortal man, and I cannot but feel as one. I have too much respect for the purity of home, too much reverence for my mother, to leave her society to pass my hours with women of the *demi-monde*. I have heard of the love you bore my father, of his devotion to you, only second to his sense of duty, in obedience to which he, with a noble heroism, sacrificed his life. Do not grudge me similar happiness. I have wealth enough to choose a portionless girl, if she be worthy of your son. I would not have her inferior to my mother, yet where shall I find her equal?"

Lady Yorke touched his well-developed brow with her lips, and smiled.

"I will, as far as I can, lay aside every unjust prejudice with regard to this young lady, and judge her as I would myself be judged."

"I am content," replied Eustace; "and now I depart for the North. A month will give you a tolerable means of judging, if you can prevail on her people to let her stay with you at Elm Hall. At the end of that time I will return, and try my fortune, if you approve—if not, I will prolong my stay till her return to her home."

In pursuance of this scheme, Lady Yorke determined to call on Constance's stepmother, and trust to chance for some means of carrying out her plans, and carrying off

Miss Rivers to Lady Yorke's country residence.

Mrs. Rivers had on that morning resigned herself to the infliction of an old schoolfellow—Mrs. Mag, the mother of Theophilus Mag, formerly introduced to the reader.

Mrs. Mag, less pretentious than Mrs. Rivers, had been contented to continue to reside in the City; and, as a reward, Mr. Mag had indulged her with a country house on the Peckham Rye, to which suburban retreat they fled from the smoke and suffocation of Castle Square.

This gave her an advantage over Mrs. Rivers, who, when she proposed a stay at Margate or Ramsgate during the autumn, was reproached by her husband with the expense of a house at the West End, and seldom succeeded in inhaling sea breezes, or, as she said, in " getting a sniff of the briny," without more trouble to coax Mr. R. into a good temper than the whole affair was worth. Mrs. Mag had come voluntarily to spend the day with her old school-fellow, as she wanted to do some shopping in Town.

Had Mrs. Rivers anticipated the visit of such an aristocrat as Lady Yorke, she would have been denied to Mary Mag, as she called her; but with the ordinary run of callers at No. 36 Mrs. Mag was on a par.

CHAPTER V.

"Souvenirs de jeune âge,
Sont gravés dans mon cœur,
Et je pense au village,
Pour rêver de bonheur."

WHEN Lady Yorke was announced by the servant, Mrs. Mag did not catch her name; but Mrs. Rivers heard the title, and was determined to "hold her own," and not to be put down by any "bloated aristocrat."

Mrs. Mag rose, whilst a good-tempered smile expanded itself over her large mouth, and lighted up her red and white complexion—her fubsy fin-like hands crossed over her plump figure, and made a curtsey to the new comer.

Mrs. Rivers sat still and glared at her through her spectacles. Thus Lady Yorke might be forgiven the mistake of supposing Mrs. Mag to be the mistress of the house, so she thus addressed her—

"I have the pleasure of speaking to Mrs. Rivers, I believe."

"Lawk! no," said the fat lady; "that's the mistress of the house!" and then, fearing the strange lady might, as she afterwards said, be *dashed* at her mistake, she continued, "not but what I am quite at home here— just one of the family, so your thought is quite excusable."

"Why don't you get up, Betsy, and make your manners?" (*Sotto voce.*)

This, however, was overheard by Lady Yorke, who said sweetly, turning to the immovable mistress of the house,

"I would not for the world inconvenience an invalid."

Mrs. Rivers felt this imputation too much for her patience, and she said,

" I'm perfectly well, ma'am—as strong in my limbs as you are yourself!"

Lady Yorke said she was glad to hear it, and seated herself in a chair opposite to that of her discourteous hostess. Mrs. Rivers felt much disposed to say, " What's your business here?" The seeming neglect of Sir Eustace Yorke, in not making his promised visit, had roused all her spleen, and disposed her to insult his mother; but, then, Mrs. Mag would know that the "lady" was not her usual visiting acquaintance, so she determined suddenly to be friendly with Lady Yorke, and " sit upon" her Peckham intimate. But her first rude speech weighed on her conscience, and, like the girl in the fairy-tale, who poured forth from her lips toads and vipers whenever she spoke, she could not form her utterance to produce a rose or a diamond. Nimble Mrs. Mag took advantage of the pause, and, after a glance at the delicate feet and ample train which fell in rich folds round them, she burst in—

"Come in a 'bus, mum?"

"No," said Lady Yorke, looking puzzled.

"Cab, mum?—cabs are cheats—came in a 'bus from Peckham Rye this morning—had to take a cab to come on here—gave the man sixpence. 'What's that for?' says he. 'Twasn't a yard over the mile, but he was so unpleasant. Says he, 'Old lady, you may walk for me in future—do you good—shake down those fat sides!" Yes, indeed, mum, 'fat sides' was the words. 'Like your imperence,' says I; but I gave him another sixpence to stop his mouth."

In the meantime Mrs. Rivers sat flushing all over at the very "low" information which her friend was conveying as to her domestic arrangements; and was considerably relieved when Lady Yorke, who wished to curtail her own punishment in the forced association with such ungenial companions, said sweetly,

"I had hoped for the pleasure of seeing your daughters, Mrs. Rivers—are they at home?"

"Your *ladyship*"—("Lor!" said Mrs. Mag, *sotto voce*)—"your ladyship is very good. My gals are devoted to the fine harts; and Charlotte is playing the piancrer; and Jane is with the 'Talian master; but they shall appear directly," and she rang the bell, and desired the footman to tell the young ladies that Lady Yorke desired to see them.

Good-natured Mrs. Mag, having at length closed her open mouth of astonishment at the announcement of the visitor's rank, jumped up, and, with another succession of little curtsies, said,

"I beg ten thousand pardons of your ladyship, my lady, but I didn't justly catch what James said when you came in; and as I never saw a real lady in Betsy's house before, I hope your ladyship will excuse my bad manners. Pray, is your husband a Lord, my lady, or a Baroknight?"

"My late husband was a baronet," said Lady Yorke, gravely.

"Beg pardin agin—didn't know you was a widow."

Mrs. Rivers grew redder and redder, but a diversion was made by the entrance of her daughters, at the sight of whom Lady Yorke's heart sank within her.

"Of what could Eustace be thinking when he fell in love with either of these girls!" she said to herself.

Low-browed and sallow, thick-lipped,

and clumsy in figure, the only difference between them seemed that the elder girl was more sullen, and that in the expression of the youngest there was more of *méchanceté*. The greeting with which Lady Yorke had intended to meet them died away on her lips. Poor lady! with all her love for her son, I doubt whether she would have undertaken the venture, had she been aware of all its disagreeables; and deeply enamoured as was her dutiful son, he certainly would not have required the sacrifice, had he known all its accompaniments.

"I regret to have interfered with your studies," said the lady, turning to the eldest.

"It don't signify," said Charlotte, sullenly.

Lady Yorke turned to the youngest.

"And do you like the study of the Italian language very much?"

Miss Jane wriggled herself about, putting her head down towards one shoulder, which rose to meet it, and then towards the other, and murmured something inarticulately.

"What Goths!" said the lady, mentally.

There was an awkward pause, for Mrs. Rivers could not but perceive that her children had made a bad impression on the titled visitor; but Mrs. Mag was convinced that on her alone depended the smoothness and hilarity of the meeting, and so she burst out with—

"Come, Charlotte, give us that pretty little tune you're always singing to my Mag —'I love but thee.'"

"I am sure," said Charlotte, reddening to a purple tint, "I never sing anything of that kind to Mr. Theophilus Mag."

"Don't be shy, my dear," said the imperturbable speaker—" no harm in an innicent attachment. My lady here ain't been married and a widder for nothing, you may depend." Then, in an audible whisper to Lady Yorke—" Spoons on my son—don't like to own it before your ladyship." Then, in a louder voice—" My son Theo is fond of singing. I call him my Mag, 'cause his Christen name is Theophilus, and that's a long one. They call my good man Old Mag, and my son Young Mag, and one gentleman, full of his jokes, is always saying, ' How now, mad Mag?' But I can't see why, for he's the sensiblest young man I ever saw, and I know there's nothing wrong in the heads of any of *my* side of the house. I can't answer so well for Mr. Mag, for I never heard he had any ancestors at all, seeing, my lady, he's worked his way to the top of the tree—and more credit to him, say I !"

"I quite agree with you," said Lady Yorke, cordially, thinking how refreshing was the unpretending vulgarity of Mrs. Mag, compared with the hopeless efforts made by Mrs. Rivers and her daughters to be "fine."

"I hope," said the lady, "that I shall not be deprived of the pleasure of hearing Miss Rivers sing."

"Yes, my dear, sing the song you sing so pretty to my son."

"I never sing to your son at all," said the young lady, bursting with anger at the idea that she was losing her chance of the young Baronet by the indiscreet revelations of Mrs. Mag; whilst Lady Yorke was doubtful whether Miss Rivers were really playing a double game (what a degradation, even in thought!) between her son and the son of Mrs. Mag.

With the monocular vision of a lover,

Eustace had spoken but of one lady, and that one a Miss Rivers. Thus his mother had no choice but to believe that the lady before her was the choice of her son's heart, and never before had she had such conviction of the blindness of Cupid. At length a bright thought cast a ray of hope through the gloomy confusion of her thoughts. There must be a third daughter—yet this one was introduced as *Miss* Rivers.

In the meantime Miss Charlotte had placed an Italian air on the piano, and had begun to sing, huskily, and with a villainous pronunciation. Mrs. Mag, who had been very much aggrieved by the young lady's slight to her son, left the room; and her absence was not observed, or, if seen, not regretted by the party present. She was a shrewd woman, and suspected that something to her son's disadvantage with regard to his attachment to Miss Charlotte was contemplated, and determined, as she said mentally, "to be even with them."

Lady Yorke bore the husky voice and the evil pronunciation with patience, so occupied was she with the question which quivered on her lips, and was uttered so soon as some polite thanks had rewarded the conclusion of the song.

"Have I seen *all* your family, Mrs. Rivers?"

"These two are all the girls I have," said the lady addressed, keeping within the strict letter of the truth.

Lady Yorke bowed and sighed, when the door opened, and the pudsy, good-tempered face of Mrs. Mag appeared, now flushed to a deeper glow by triumph. She led on, or rather dragged along, Constance, saying,

"Come, my dear, I don't see you've done anything to be ashamed of."

When Constance had been seduced by

Mrs. Mag to accompany her so far as the drawing-room door, where that lively old lady, fearing Constance would escape, was about to impel her onward progress by the application of a pair of fubsy hands to her shoulders, which would have made her entrance to the presence of those there assembled more sudden than dignified; but Constance, though not suspecting any scheme, was too polite to precede Mrs. Mag, and hung back, to allow the elder lady to go on, who contented herself with seizing the slender wrist of the young girl, and holding it tightly till she had dragged her into the drawing-room.

"There, Lady Yorke, there's a gal worth looking at—there's lilies and roses as don't grow in Lunnon—country-bred, country-fed; this is the *real* Miss Rivers, daughter of the first wife, whot died in childbirth, poor thing!"

Constance, flushing all over at this unusual introduction, curtsied to Lady Yorke, and said timidly to her step-mother,

" What are your commands, madam ?"

" I suppose you know yourself, as you have come without being wanted," said Mrs. Rivers, in a surly tone.

" Come, come, Betsy, don't be cantankerous—it was only a little *judy spree* of mine," said Mrs. Mag, good-naturedly—" I told her you wanted her—only a bit of a *make-believe,* you know."

Constance was about to retire, but Lady Yorke, who was interested in seeing more of one who had attracted her son, said, moving a few steps forward,

" Pray do not let me lose the pleasure which this lady has so kindly contrived for my gratification—unless, indeed, you have some occupation so interesting, that you grudge me a few moments of your time."

Constance raised her deep blue eyes timidly, and, blushing still more, said,

"My time is of no consequence—my occupation consists only in watering the mignonette in the boxes outside the window, and in feeding the sparrows with crumbs collected from the luncheon-table. I miss the pets I used to gather round me in the country, where I have lived all my life till within the last few weeks," she said sadly.

"Beggars mustn't be choosers," said Mrs. Rivers; "you may be glad to have a good house over your head, and nothing to pay, and no harder work than watering flowers and feeding sparrows."

The flush passed from Constance's face to that of Lady Yorke, at this cruel taunt. This lady was silent from disgust at the ill-breeding shown by Mrs. Rivers. As knights of old never tilted but with those of their own degree, and left their squires to wage battle with squires, Lady Yorke felt that she could not mix in a war of words with a woman at once cruel and vulgar; but whilst the chivalrous lady declined, the one of lower grade rushed into the strife with right good will.

"Never you mind, my dear," to Constance; "some folks hate a pretty face like pison. I've got a sweet little willy by the side of the high road—busses every hour to and from Lunnon. You shall be welcome to live with Sam and me so long as you like —no stint—roast meat at two o'clock every day, and a nice hot supper at nine—ale or wine just as you like, or a glass of hot brandy and water—that's *my* sort." In a whisper, "I'll pay your washing, my dear— I can't bear to see folks put upon—and you won't be dull; Mag brings down some nice young men every Saturday till Monday, and who knows what may happen? So never mind snubbings here—you'll always be welcome to me and Sam."

Thus spoke the good dame, urged alike by a desire to revenge herself on the family of the second Mrs. Rivers, for the slight offered to her darling son; and by pity for the gentle girl, whose eyes were filled with tears at her stepmother's words.

She thanked Mrs. Mag in faltering accents, neither accepting nor declining her cordial invitation, and an awkward silence fell on the party—Mrs. Rivers being ashamed of her violence, which had not been a success, as it showed how much sympathy it had excited for her step-daughter; her daughters being provoked by Constance's appearance on the scene; and Lady Yorke being perplexed how to make a good graceful retreat from a set of people so uncongenial. A knock at the door relieved them all from a situation so embarrassing, and a few moments after Mr. Rivers entered.

"Thank heaven! a gentleman at last!—at least in appearance," she thought, as he entered the room, with his milk-white hair waving over a well-shaped forehead, and the absence of pretension in his manner which is in itself so great a charm. He bowed to the strange lady, on whom refinement was written in unmistakable characters, rather puzzled to know how she could be found in juxtaposition with his wife, but pleased to accept the situation.

"Lady Yorke, will you permit me to introduce my father to your ladyship?" said Constance, after looking vainly towards Mrs. Rivers, in the expectation of her doing this act of courtesy.

"Is there any news?" said her ladyship, looking at the paper in the hand of Mr. Rivers, as they exchanged salutations.

" Ladies only care for the *Morning Post*," said Mr. Rivers smiling; "and we City men prefer the *Daily News*, as giving us the most reliable money-market intelligence."

"Ah! but in these times," replied the lady, "such subjects come home to every woman's business and bosom, as well as every man's—as Madame de Staël said—if women have to lose their heads, it's natural they should wish to know the reason why—if women are to lose their balance at their banker's, the money article and City intelligence must possess the liveliest interest to them."

It was not often that Mr. Rivers found a lady possessed both of grace and intelligence, willing to converse with him. He began to explain the City article, eagerly and clearly, walking into the back drawing-room, where the table, generally covered with Miss Jane's Italian books, stood now temptingly empty for the outstretched sheet of the *Daily News*, down which his forefinger travelled slowly, as he continued his explanations.

Lady Yorke was interested in the information he conveyed, but was more intent in making a favourable impression, that she might carry the point on which the heart of Eustace was intent. In the meantime, Mrs. Rivers sat swelling with indignation at the various mortifications to which she conceived she had been subjected, and which, in her innermost mind, she determined to revenge on Constance the first available opportunity.

Her daughters, who felt vaguely that they had not made a favourable impression on their new visitor, whom, as the mother of Sir Eustace, they wished to propitiate, shared her internal discontent, and her external sullenness. Mrs. Mag prattled cheerfully to Constance, who, scared at having been the cause of looks so very black and words so very insulting on the part of her relatives, could scarcely give the necessary rejoinders to her good-natured champion.

At length Lady Yorke took advantage of a pause in the conversation with Mr. Rivers, to compliment him on his happiness in having three charming daughters.

"If Heaven had so blest me," said her ladyship, with a little sigh, "I should not be so companionless in my solitude."

The little sigh was *made* to account for the speech that was to follow; for Lady Yorke felt that Eustace filled every corner of her heart, and had never in fancy found room for another.

"You have a very gallant son, I understand, Lady Yorke. I remember his having received the Cross for valour."

"Ah! true; but laurels cannot be won in our own gardens, and most of my son's life has been spent in distant lands. I am now about to return to my lonely country house. Do you not think that you could spare Miss Rivers to spend a week or ten days with me in my seclusion. My son is in the Highlands, and I have little amusement to offer; but I will take every care of your daughter, if she will consent to accompany me."

Lady Yorke had rightly read the flush of gratified pride which passed over the father's face at this proposition.

"Your ladyship is very good," he said. "Constance, come here. Lady Yorke says she will kindly be burthened by your company for a few days in the country."

Constance gave a timid look of assent, and her lips formed the monosyllable "when?" though no sound proceeded from them. In truth, the appearances of threatening storms on the part of the Rivers' ladies made her eager to escape as soon as possible—a feeling which Lady Yorke understood, but to which Mr. Rivers had no clue.

"I should be only too delighted could Miss Rivers accompany me at once—could you?" turning to Constance.

Constance looked at her father for permission.

"Certainly, my dear. I will send your wardrobe, if you will give orders as to what you require. Go and put on your bonnet; and as I was saying, my lady, that, depressed as the money market is at present, I hope Sir Eustace will not, &c., &c."

Constance had left by the door of the back drawing-room, not to be questioned by her step-mother, and re-appeared in a few minutes in her bonnet and cloak.

"Go down," said her father, hastily. "I will explain to your mother, and make your adieus to her and to your sisters."

He was fearful of his wife's violence, and wished to avoid a scene. Mrs. Mag, finding her position untenable, after Constance had left the room, had "hoped she should find Betsy Rivers in a better mind next time," and had walked down and opened the front door without the honours of war, which she certainly had deserved. Constance had wished to press the hand of the kind woman before she left the house, for the expressions of her gratitude had fallen cramped from her lips by the malign presence in which they were uttered. She remembered, however, the address of the "sweet willy," and determined to write a note of thanks for the hospitality so frankly offered.

Lady Yorke made her farewells to the

ladies with less than her previous cordiality. Her ladyship disliked them more for the forced contact in which she had been placed with them. Besides, she had succeeded in carrying off Constance without their consent, or even their cognizance, and felt she had nothing more to gain. Mr. Rivers attended her to the door with respect the most profound. He had just handed her ladyship and Constance into the carriage, and stood bowing, to receive the last smile from its occupants, when, as it drove off, Theophilus Mag swaggered up the steps on which Mr. Rivers was standing.

"My governess here?" said the young man, conscious of a mutual dislike existing between himself and the person whom he addressed.

"The ladies are all in the drawing-room —you had better go in and see," said the father, wishing to get rid of the youth himself, whilst he retired to the back dining-room, called his study, not unwilling to put off the evil hour of explanation with his wife as to Constance's absence.

"O mihi beate Martini!" said Theophilus, bounding up three stairs at a time—which is, being interpreted, "O my eye and Betty Martin!"—"how we apples swim! Grand doings, when such a really lady visits here! What a pair of splendid carriage 'osses—saw worse ones go at Tats for three hundred and fifty pounds!"

When he opened the drawing-room door, Mrs. Rivers was still swelling with vexation, but he thought it was with the dignity reflected from her departed visitor.

"Sweet woman!—grand creature!—isn't she?" said he, apostrophising Lady Yorke, but addressing his hostess, to give the idea that he was himself intimately acquainted with her. "Known her long?"

Mrs. Rivers determined to make the most of the situation.

"Well, not very long," recollecting that Mrs. Mag had been present during part of the interview. "Not very long; but there is a probability that we shall be *very* intimate in future. In fact, 'tis a thing not to be talked about at present. But the son of her ladyship—young Baronet, magnificent fortune!—has been very much struck—smitten, I may say—by the attractions of Charlotte; and her ladyship had a long conversation with Mr. Rivers in the back drawing-room, and no doubt with reference to the necessary arrangements."

The brow of Theophilus darkened. He had frequently bestowed the honour of his attention on this young lady, and though he had never gravely intended to commit himself to marriage, the notion of her being carried off by a wealthy young Baronet was too much for his equanimity. The young lady sat by, gloomy and repulsive to her former admirer. But Theophilus was a sharp youth, and he remembered the vision of a fair creature smiling happily by the side of Lady Yorke, and he thought,

"This is a dodge of the old lady's to bring me to book. I don't believe a word of the story."

However, he determined to give all seeming credence to the words of his hostess, and put on a look of deep depression, whilst he cast down his glances, lest the fun that danced in them should sparkle from under their lids. He sidled to a chair next to that which held his charmer, determined to see whether the praises he had bestowed on Lady Yorke had piqued the younger lady's jealousy, and inclining his head languishingly towards her, he passed his arm round the back of her chair—a frequent custom of his.

"If she likes me," he argued, "she will—*unconsciously, of course*—lean back. If she means mischief, she will sit bolt upright!"

Alas! the plump high shoulders held themselves intact from the offered embrace, and the gentleman became both puzzled and disturbed. He did not much care for Miss Rivers, but she seemed to rise in value now that it seemed she was about to escape from his power of appropriation.

"I suppose," said Theophilus, "you haven't a word for a poor fellow like me, now you are after a baronet?"

"Pray do not be so coarse," said Mrs. Rivers; "my daughter is not *after* any one. I said Sir Eustace seemed smitten with Charlotte, and (simpering) I have good reason to know that Lady Yorke did not stay so long in the back drawing-room with Mr. R. for nothing."

"Well, hang me if I can understand it,"

said Mag, junior; "what the deuce did she mean by carrying away the wrong one, then?"

"What do you mean, sir?" said both ladies in a breath, and breathlessly.

"Why, I mean the pretty little pullet by the first hatch."

"I don't understand you," screamed Mrs. Rivers.

"Well, there she was, like a chicken under the wing of a magnificent hen, who seemed wonderfully proud of her, and inclined to 'cluck' in the exuberance of delight at having her safe at her side; and you know (musingly), Miss Rivers *is* a beautiful girl—every one must allow *that*."

Now, before Constance's advent, Charlotte had always been called "Miss Rivers," and the familiar title, coupled with the term beautiful, called a smile over the face of the muddy-skinned girl, from old association.

This faded in the perturbation occasioned by her perplexity as to Mag's meaning; but a happy thought came to the relief of Mrs. Rivers, to which she gave utterance.

"Mr. Theophilus Mag," she said, "no one can be more aware than my daughter and myself of your powers of hoaxing. It is very charming sometimes, but at present Miss Rivers and I have much to think of, and if you will call again another day we shall be able better to appreciate your funning. I wish you a good afternoon," and she rose and made a formal curtsey.

"Ah!" thought Mag. "I have thrown a hand-grenade into their camp. Mrs. R., your humble; Miss Charlotte, though cruel, yet I am your devoted Like a well-bred dog I take my departure, fearing a final kick; but should my expectations prove correct, and your chance of the title be a delusion and a snare, why, whistle, and I *won't* come to you, my love. Good day, ladies," and he bowed, laughing maliciously, and withdrew.

"Really, that young man is intolerable, Charlotte—he has quite flustered me with his nonsense—so under-bred!"

"Yes," said the young lady, slowly; "but there is something I didn't quite like in his looks—mortified and jealous, probably," she added, with a little air of importance, "and, therefore, spiteful. I can easily get him round again whenever I like; but, really, if Sir Eustace *does* think of me, I would rather he kept out of the way—Sir Eustace might not like his manner—ahem!—to his future wife," and she briddled and smirked at the idea of being Lady Yorke.

It seems strange to find how completely a man superior to his wife in every respect may be held in subjection from dread of her violence. Probably the loss of domestic peace, from the family barometer pointing to "stormy," prevents many a worthy man from doing what is both right and agreeable to himself.

Mr. Rivers had been flattered by Lady Yorke's invitation to his eldest daughter. She was, whilst in the house, a constant source of grumbling to his wife; yet now he had, without consulting his worse half, consented to Constance's absence, he rather dreaded the scene which would take place when the fact became known.

In fact, Constance was the safety-valve for all her step-mother's ill-tempers. She was metaphorically flogged for the faults of others, as was the unhappy boy kept to undergo vicarious punishment for the Dauphin of France. The infliction of pain was a positive pleasure when Constance was the recipient of it; so Mr. Rivers, dreading the avalanche of his wife's wrath, said nothing as the family descended, without Constance, to the dining-room.

"Umph! Miss Rivers does not seem ready—bad manners, *I* consider it. Ring the bell and send Martha to Miss Rivers' room, to desire her to come to dinner."

The footman hesitated, and looked at his master. Had he not stood himself, and opened the street-door, and witnessed the exit of both ladies? "Why don't master speak?" was the thought of James the footman.

Master was ladling out the soup with such care and exactitude that it seemed he was counting each separate tube of the vermicelli that hung from the silver ladle. James, receiving no aid from the higher powers, gasped out,

"'Taint no use to send Martha upstairs, 'cause Miss Constance's not in the house."

"Not in the house!" screamed the lady.

"Calm yourself, my dear," said Mr. Rivers; "Constance has gone to spend a few days with Lady Yorke."

"Brute!—monster!" shrieked the lady. "I am despised, set at nought in my own house! Ah! that was *it*—the hen!" she screamed.

"The pullet!" re-echoed Charlotte sobbing. "I knew he was making game of us."

"Making game of us, indeed!" rejoined Mrs. Rivers; "but 'tis all your father's fault —insulting me so—I who have been *such* a wife!"

"D——n it, what's all this about!" said Mr. Rivers, with the deep bass of his voice, coming like the growl of an enraged lion. "Surely I'm master of my own house?" said he, rising and stamping with indignation, "and Constance shall go where she likes, and stay where she likes. I only wish the other members of my household were as sweet-tempered, and amiable, and *beautiful* —yes, BEAUTIFUL, as she is!"

As he gave utterance to these fearful words, Mrs. Rivers threw herself back in her chair, and began to kick and pant, after the fashion of ladies working up a fit of hysterics.

Her daughters ministered to her supposed necessities, and Mr. Rivers, rising and seizing the moderator lamp, walked with it into his study, and desired James to lay the cloth there, and bring the rest of the dinner, not to *disturb* Mrs. Rivers.

"There is no reason why I should lose my dinner because she is in such a temper," he thought.

So alternately reading a sentence in the *Times*, and taking a mouthful of soup, he enjoyed himself thoroughly, and forgot there was an enraged wife, who, having exhausted tears and sobs, now "wrapt in grim repose," awaited her "evening prey." Nemesis often lurks behind the curtains of the matrimonial couch.

Nothing was seen of the youthful Mag for three weeks, at the end of which period there was a grand horticultural fête, whither in former days he would have accompanied Mrs. Rivers and her daughters. No news, either, of Sir Eustace had been received. So Mrs. Rivers enclosed a ticket to Mr. Theophilus Mag, with her best regards. It was returned with a polite note, saying he had been already supplied with one.

"He is sure to join our party when he sees me," said Miss Charlotte.

"Well! I hope he may," said the less sanguine mother. "It is very awkward to have no young man—indeed, no men, either old or young, to escort us."

The day arrived, and Miss Charlotte and her sister were dressed in straw-coloured sarsnet covered with lace, and white silk bonnets, adorned with full-blown roses. They walked about till the tightening of their lilac boots, put on new for the occasion, made every fresh step a source of irritation and misery, for their feet were clumsy and thick, and their boots were narrow and pointed. Their mother had nearly expended the patience of which the maternal stock seems almost inexhaustible, and no gentleman joined them. They had not met Mag.

"Something has prevented his coming," said Miss Charlotte.

Mrs. Rivers cared little for the flowers —the young ladies cared less. It is said that "when matters come to the worst they will certainly mend." The difficulty is to know when that interesting crisis has arrived.

Perhaps the clouds took pity on the poor toes that swelled and glowed on the hot gravel. They certainly melted into drops, both heavy and frequent. The fair creatures, mindful of silk slips, spotless muslins, and summer bonnets, rushed about in all directions to get to the tents. If the nearest were full, they made an effort for the next. Many a lover sank in the estimation of his fair one, by showing more anxiety for the preservation of his superfine cloth than for her gauze bonnet and lace veil.

Selfishness peeped out unexpectedly, and many a promising flirtation ended in a fit of sulk. But the pain which caused separation of tender hearts also brought them in some cases into closer contact. Storms have been propitious ever since the days of Queen Dido. Miss Charlotte had been separated from her mother and sister in the first violence of the shower; they having bolted in opposite directions. The tent where Miss Charlotte sought refuge was so filled, that there was some difficulty in getting so far within its shelter as to avoid the streams which poured down from the edge of the saturated canvas.

But there she stood—safe, but companionless, as to acquaintance, and with ample time to contemplate the wet and soiled hem of her dress, and the long torn loops of lace which depended from it. Some one had trodden on it—perhaps she had done it herself in her flight. She began to feel lonely. Other girls were laughing and talking with their " young men ;" she had no one to speak to. She wondered where was Theophilus—why had he kept away?

The fickle sun streamed out in all his glory, and the ladies put first one, and then the other, delicate foot on the wet gravel, and leaned on the arms of their companions as they left the tent.

"Oh! I'm so tired!—I'll sit down when the tent is cleared," thought Charlotte.

The tent at length emptied—no, not quite. Just at the extreme end a couple were seated, so engrossed with each other, that they did not see that they were nearly alone. The lady was young and pretty, and beautifully dressed. Charlotte knew her to be the daughter and heiress of a wealthy dry-salter. She knew the position of the gentleman—the arm round the back of the chair; she recognized the single broad stripe of the trousers, and she could bear the sight no longer, but hobbled out over the saturated gravel, and sat down on the first seat despondingly, resolving to wait till her mother should find her, and sagely determining that reunion would be best promoted by one party remaining stationary.

At length the forlorn ladies were reunited, and were bent on going home at once; but, alas! how should they attain their carriage? They were ready to cry with vexation. After entreating unavailingly one attendant after another to find their footman, or to call Mrs. Rivers' carriage, they were obliged to apply to Theophilus, whom they saw passing with the young lady on his arm, and who promised to return and attend to them in a few minutes, as soon as he had escorted Miss Hammond to hers. That charming girl, having been listening to the playful accents of Theophilus in the recesses of the tent before the storm began, was uninjured by rain or splashes of yellow gravel. Her bonnet of white crape, ornamented by a single rose-bud, admitted a softened light over her pretty countenance, whilst the thick white silk of those of the Miss Rivers contrasted painfully with their muddy complexions. The petals of their roses were glued together by the wet, and the green leaves had discharged their colour in long streaks over the crown and front of their head-gear. All this pressed on the discouraged feelings of Miss Charlotte in a moment of time as she saw Miss Hammond in passing.

"Oh! mamma, 'tis your fault entirely!" she said; but finding that she must cry if she proceeded, and seeing the single stripe trousers making their way back through the crowd, she was silent, whilst Theophilus gave his arm to Mrs. Rivers, and she followed with her sister.

As the door of the carriage was about to be closed, Theophilus leant towards her, with a beaming face of fun. She bent to hear him with a ready smile of forgiveness, not doubting but that the coming whisper would contain an overture of reconciliation, but heard only—"How about the Baronet!" concluding with a mocking laugh.

Miss Charlotte sank back as the carriage proceeded, and sobbed bitterly, recovering herself only to reproach her mother, in the same breath, for having chosen for her a thick instead of a transparent bonnet, and for having deluded her with false hopes of obtaining Sir Eustace. One consolation she had—and it was great—she released her feet from durance, and tried to dry and warm them in the rug at the bottom of the carriage, whilst Mrs. Rivers determined to give Mr. Rivers " a bit of her mind," as to the impropriety of his not attending them abroad—forgetting that from his exertions in the City came the carriage, horses, silk bonnets, and tight lilac boots.

When Lady Yorke looked round on her

companion in the carriage, she felt genuine admiration for the beauty of the young lady. What lovely dark blue eyes!—what lashes! —what a delicate skin!—slender—too narrow across the shoulders, rather!—consumptive! That would not do for Eustace. His wife must be healthy.

"My dear Miss Rivers, is there too much air? Shall I draw up the window on my side?" the lady said, almost with tenderness.

"Oh! dear, no," said Constance. "I cannot have too much fresh air. It seems to me that I have been undergoing a course of stifling lately!"

The lady looked at the young girl, and she returned the gaze, though timidly. The smile with which Lady Yorke had spoken remained fixed on her face, but the reference to Constance's paternal home had awakened unpleasant thoughts in Lady Yorke's mind, which were to this tenor—" Can any good thing come out of Galilee?"

Constance was silent also; but her thoughts went no deeper than, "I wonder if Mary will put up my clothes and send them?"

Mary was the housemaid, who had been more than usually attentive to Constance, because servants often feel a rude sense of justice, which makes them anxious to smooth the paths of those who are "put upon" by their betters, and because she hated the ladysmaid, who was the chosen companion of Mrs. Rivers and the other two young ladies.

The doubt about Mary's fulfilment of Constance's request brought a look of perplexity over her face, which Lady Yorke detected at once.

"What is it?"

"Madam?"

"What is worrying you?"

"Oh!" said Constance, honestly, "I was not worried—that is, not much; but I was only thinking whether my wardrobe would be sent. I did not pack my clothes myself, lest I should keep your ladyship waiting."

"Never mind; if they do not come, we will send for them—or you shall have anything you want from me; and as we are not going to ride a race, we need not fear for my clothes the fate of the hat and wig lent to John Gilpin by the callender; and, I may say with him, 'My clothes are twice the size of yours, therefore they needs must fit.' My maid might easily 'take in' a dress or two of mine for your use."

The ease with which Lady Yorke met difficulties gave Constance the conviction that wealth and placid temper are great sweeteners of life. With what exclamations of anger and annoyance would Constance have been greeted had she by any chance lost her luggage on first arriving in town, and been compelled to apply to her stepsisters for a loan of linen.

Her anxieties were unfounded, however. Before Lady Yorke had returned from her drive round the park, Constance's trunk and boxes had arrived, thanks to the stringent orders of her father, and the exertions of Mary the housemaid.

After dinner Lady Yorke asked if she would like to go to the Opera, to which Constance of course assented, adding that it would be a novelty to her—she had never been to any place of public amusement. Lady Yorke was satisfied with her beautiful *protégée*, whose appearance caused curiosity and admiration amongst even those whose taste is made fastidious by its being constantly exercised on the most admirable and the most refined. She was pleased, too, by Constance's enjoyment of the music; it was so genuine, and free from grimace.

CHAPTER VI.

"Birds, flowers, soft winds and waters gently flowing,
  Surround me day and night,
Still sweetly on my heart bestowing
  Content and calm delight.
When day's toil wearies, sleep my peace restoring,
  Descends with balmy night—
In bright dreams on my bosom pouring
  Content and calm delight."
                                   HERCULES ELLIS.

ON the following day Lady Yorke started for Elm Hall. Constance was silent on the journey, her mind being full of expectation; but, on arriving, she gave way to all the enthusiasm and delight of girlhood.

"Oh! what a fine old place!—what a magnificent avenue!—what a lovely piece of water!—how grand the trees look reflected in it! Oh! Lady Yorke, what new life you have given me by bringing me hither!"

As she walked through the picture-gallery, she looked at some choice specimens of ancient art, and named the painters as she passed, in most instances with correctness, though they lacked the friendly black letters on the gold frames, which show the visitors what they are expected to consider them—Reubens, Vandyck, Velasquez, is it? timidly.

"Ah! there is a Hobbina!"

"How do you know?"

"I spent nearly all my life—all excepting a few months at school—with my mother; I mean my adopted mother—no, my foster-mother—I was her adopted child, in a house which contained many pictures. I heard who painted them from my mother, who used to show them to visitors; and from looking at them in every possible variety of lights—from the cold morning hours to the broad light of noon and the glow of sunset, I learnt to recognise the different painters. I loved them all; and every month I fancied I discovered something I had never seen before—some meaning I had not before understood."

"And did you never try to imitate them?"

"Oh! no. Had I seen a simple outline of a house, or a tree, or an animal, I might have tried to copy it; but I should as soon have thought of trying to build an old mansion like Boscobel as to imitate one of the paintings on its walls."

"It seems a pity that you were not taught."

"There were no masters to be had in that remote part of Cornwall; and had there been, there would not have been—" she was going to say the money to pay for one, but she stopped, for it seemed a reflection on Mr. Rivers. Lady Yorke still looked inquiringly.

"A certain sum was allowed for my maintenance when I was an infant. I think my father never thought of increasing it, and my foster-mother was too much afraid of losing me to remind Mr. Rivers that a girl of nineteen requires more than an infant of nine days old."

With this Constance dismissed the subject. On the subject of ornithology she was as well instructed as in pictures. She named the birds in their stuffed cases, both native and foreign. In explanation, she said,

"My foster-mother's father is gamekeeper at Boscobel. When I was quite a little girl he used to show me the pictures in 'Bewick's Birds.' I learnt all about them, because I had nothing else to do. As I grew older, I found in the library accounts of foreign birds, with beautiful pictures—Audubon's amongst the rest. It is much easier to add a little every day to a store of which one has a little, than to try to accumulate where there is no foundation—no nest egg, as it were, of knowledge."

"She is quite intelligent enough," thought Lady Yorke, "if she be but refined and sincere. Tell me about your foster-mother, Constance?"

"For the last eight years of her life she was very quiet—it was her nature to be silent at all times; but she suffered from disease of the heart latterly, and she used to sit up in an arm-chair, and get me to read to her all day long. In the morning I read the Psalms, Lessons, Epistle, and Gospel of the day. I used to consider that as the duty part of the work; when that had been accomplished, I used to read other things."

"What?"

"Oh! my lady, old-fashioned books you would not care to read about—'The Spectator,' that wonderful gentleman whose face grew so unnaturally short from his never speaking; 'The Rambler'—'The World.' I used to fancy my mother was Lady Bountiful—for though not rich, she was always doing good."

"And you used to read these books aloud constantly?"

"Yes, whenever I could."

"I suppose that accounts for your language being more than ordinarily good?"

"Is it?" said Constance. "I am sure I am very glad; but I did not know it. I used to like to read about the ladies in the *Spectator*, because, looking down the long picture-gallery, I could fancy them stepping down from their walls and flirting their fans till the powder flew from the ample wigs of their beaux."

"Did you like the gamekeeper?—your mother's father, who showed you the pictures in Bewick."

"Not quite," said Constance, shortly; and then flushing, as if conscious of ill-breeding, she forced a smile and said, "I liked him when I was quite a child; but somehow he altered a great deal as I grew older. My mother was devoted to him."

"He must have been a very old man."

"About sixty. Poor father! Yes, I must have loved him very much," she continued, musing. "My mother was but forty when she died," said Constance, with tearful eyes.

Lady Yorke liked her young companion; whether she was worthy of Eustace she dared not decide as yet, but she was very agreeable to her.

Lady Yorke happened to say one day that she had a partiality to mushrooms, and the next morning Constance went out "o'er the dewy green" at six o'clock, and brought in a basket full of those pearls of the turf.

"There!" she said, triumphantly, as they came in simmering in their silver dish. " I cooked them myself!—and, oh! Lady Yorke, if you would but let me have a sirloin of beef, I will make you the best pie you ever tasted!"

Lady Yorke laughed in spite of herself.

" How came the cook to allow any interference in her kitchen?" she asked.

" Oh! I got the kitchen-maid to bring what I wanted into the laundry. There was no linen there, being Monday, so I performed my cooking operations undisturbed."

The mushrooms were excellent. Lady Yorke did full justice to their novel treatment, and though she doubted whether

Eustace's wife should have such an accomplishment, she was not sorry to reap the benefit of it. She made Constance read to her, and had a new enjoyment in her favourite authors, from seeing how the fresh young mind of the girl appreciated them, looking on with the sad pleasure with which Louis XI. regarded Quentin Durward's insatiable appetite for venison pasty—it was an enjoyment for which neither the King nor the elder lady could share in the same degree.

Lady Yorke wrote twice a week to her son, and heard from him constantly. She did not tell him how much she liked Constance; it would be premature, she thought. She shut herself up in her own room when she wrote to him, and seized and pocketed his precious letters, with a vague fear that Constance might say something about them, forgetting that as she had not seen his handwriting, she must be utterly ignorant from whom they came.

Eustace, with the fallacy which attributes to the object of affection every taste and perception which was in himself, became quite eloquent in his description of the scenes through which he travelled, and the small adventures which he encountered in his journey. How could he tell that

> "The pomp of groves, the garniture of fields—
> All that the mountain's sheltering bosom shields,"

would be anything more than "leather and prunella" to Constance, had Lady Yorke shown Eustace's letters to her. That she would do this, he calculated from the impulsive habit she had of throwing her letters to him across the breakfast-table. As it was, the eloquence never went beyond Lady Yorke's breast. Sometimes she felt provoked at the little interest Constance evinced in that one subject of Sir Eustace, when on every other she seemed to fling herself into all that concerned her hostess with more than the eagerness of youth.

She had just glanced at a full-length portrait of him in the gallery in uniform, and covered with decorations, and then walked on to look at one of Sir Wildred Yorke, in flowing curls and breast-plate, of the year 1582. No second look was given to the representation of the handsome young living warrior.

"What extraordinary insensibility!" thought Lady Yorke.

She had never before, since her girlhood, been blessed with female society, and in Constance she felt its full charm—women get on together so much better than men and women. Then she tried to picture to herself how she should feel if Constance were the wife of Eustace. Constance was walking up and down the terrace in front of the house. Lady Yorke fancied what her sensations would be if Eustace were walking by the side of Constance, bending his graceful head towards her in a whispered conversation. No—she should then be shut out from her son's heart—she should be second then where she had always hitherto been first; and Constance, too, seemingly so fond of her now—she would love Eustace to her own exclusion. Yet Eustace would be sure to marry. There was no simpering young lady-like grimaces, no look of feminine consciousness, when Lady Yorke experimentally spoke of her son to Constance. She certainly had no scheme for catching Sir Eustace, whatever other girls might wish or plot against his liberty.

Sometimes Lady Yorke tried to lead her to speak of her first interview with Eustace, but Constance flushed so deeply, and seemed so thoroughly miserable at the recollection, that her hostess desisted.

"I was travelling alone, and a man was very insolent to me, and I put my head out of the window and screamed, and your son came, and the man ran away."

This was all the explanation. There seemed more pain in the remembrance of the insult than pleasure in the recollection of the liberator. So Lady Yorke asked no more.

One day her ladyship was entering household expenses in an account-book. She called Constance to explain to her how perfect it was in all its details, concluding with—

"I will give you one when you marry."

"I shall never marry," said Constance, quietly, but rather sadly.

"All young ladies say so till they are asked," said her ladyship.

"Perhaps I shall not be asked," she replied, with a forced smile.

Constance on one occasion was seeking a lost volume of Hookham's for the returning book-box, in a small dressing-room next to Lady Yorke's bed-room, where her favourite maid generally sat. This woman was weeping bitterly, rocking herself backwards and forwards in her chair, and with her apron thrown over her face. She did not see Constance till the young girl had seated herself by her side. "What has vexed you, nurse?" she said, kindly. "Can I do anything for you? Shall I speak to Lady Yorke?"

"I suppose, miss, I've a tongue in my head, and I can speak to my lady myself, if I choose, seeing I knowed her afore you was born," said the nurse, jealously.

"I'm very sorry for your trouble, and I should have been glad to have helped you, if I could," said Constance.

"You can't help me, nor no one else," said the nurse, "so long as that Pagan black fellow is kept here to make mischief, and take the bread out of Christians' mouths!"

Constance felt that the mischief was beyond her department, and quietly left the room; but the nurse was grateful for her sympathy, though she did not express it, and "made a note of it," for future reference.

CHAPTER VII.

"Tender-handed stroke a nettle,
And 'twill sting you for your pains.
* * * * *
"'Tis the way with vulgar natures,
Treat them kindly—they rebel."

WHEN Constance saw Lady Yorke, she spoke of the nurse's trouble, in the hope that it might be rectified by the kind mistress of the mansion. Her ladyship knew all about it, evidently, for she expressed no surprise.

"Yes," she said, meditatively, "I made a mistake common to young housekeepers, when I had been but a short time married. I took as a nurse-girl the daughter of my husband's coachman. Mistake 1. I liked her, and she was very fond of Eustace, and generally well conducted; and after Eustace left the nursery for school, I kept her to attend on myself. A few years since my groom left me to become coachman in another family, and I was then induced, by the representations of my old coachman, and of my maid, to take his grandson, who is, of course, also her nephew, in the groom's place. Mistake 2."

"Why a mistake?" said Constance. "Surely, if you are well served by one servant, it is natural to suppose that you will be equally so by one of their stock."

"Yes, I reasoned thus, but it is fallacious. Human nature is prone to err, and servants make it a point to stand by each other— by 'their order;' and ten times stronger is the feeling when it is strengthened by ties of blood. I cannot make out what Kali

Khan means by his broken English complaints, but I never liked the countenance of the groom, and I suspect those complaints will be discovered to be well-founded. I cannot dismiss the coachman, who is old, and given to drinking, because he has belonged to the family forty years. I cannot dismiss Eustace's nurse, though I believe she connives at the ill-doings of the groom; but him I am determined to dismiss, so soon as Eustace returns—this will be in about ten days' time. Nurse must reconcile herself to the inevitable results of James's misconduct, if that misconduct be proved."

That evening Lady Yorke lingered long on the upland of the park, looking with Constance at the magnificent sunset which bathed the landscape in a golden glow, and then melted into mist. Both were silent, till the girl suggested that the lake had become shrouded with fog, and that it had filled the valley through which they must return to the house.

Lady Yorke made light of the risk of cold, and declined to take off her damp dress on her going home. Before the time came for their going to bed, she had begun to shiver, and a sharp attack of fever seized her during the night. In the morning she sent the maid to Constance's room, with a request that Constance would read prayers to the household, and then make the breakfast.

Constance brought the cup of tea herself to Lady Yorke's bedside after she had complied with her other suggestion, and was shocked to see the heavy eyelids and the flushed cheeks, which told of the violence of the attack. She requested permission to send for medical attendance, to which Lady Yorke at once assented. This done, Constance obtained ice from the ice-house, and passed it over the burning scalp between the divided hair.

"Oh! Constance, that is so pleasant!" said the patient. This was the last thought with which Constance could solace herself. Before the grey dreary evening clouded in, the lady was delirious, and her mind only conveyed broken images through her parched and hurrying lips. Eustace's name was ever on her tongue.

"He ought to be sent for," said the doctor, hearing the reiteration of the name.

"Will you write, or telegraph?" said Constance timidly.

"Certainly, if you wish it—but where?"

Constance went to Watson the maid, who lifted the pincushion on the dressing-table, where Lady Yorke had concealed his letter on going to bed, and pointed out the postmark to the surgeon. He took it down, and left the room for the purpose of sending it. Then Constance looked at the map and at Bradshaw, and tried to calculate when the telegram would be received, and how soon after Sir Eustace might arrive, and relieve her of some of the responsibility of the watching.

She had attended the sick-bed of her foster-mother through more than twelve months of that anxiety which is the most dispiriting because unattended by hope, but the sickness was placid. It required rest and quiet, and the sufferer, provided no external circumstances disturbed her diseased heart, was tranquil and even cheerful, till the paroxysm was brought on by anxiety or sudden noises.

In Lady Yorke's case the danger was imminent, and the surgeon, before Eustace could arrive, asked Constance whether he might call in further advice. Of course *he* could treat the case perfectly well, but he must say he was very doubtful of the result, and friends would think perhaps that all had not been done!

"Oh! send for anyone—everyone you can think of," said Constance, in her desperation; "of course Sir Eustace would wish it."

So a consultation was decided on, and the three doctors agreed that Mr. Johnson's treatment of the case had been perfectly judicious, &c., as Mr. Johnson had fully intended they should agree, when he sent for them.

At length, about eleven o'clock one night, Constance thought she heard the distant sound of carriage wheels. The bells were muffled. "I wonder if the servants will hear him," she said. Eustace had not given them a chance—he dismissed the fly without driving up to the house, and entered by the back door. In a few minutes he stood in all the sickness of doubt at the door of his mother's bedroom, leaning against the doorsill, and contemplating the scene it contained. There she lay, jerking her head restlessly from one side to another, whilst the rest of her body seemed immovable; a wet rag was on her head, and a slight girl stood with her back turned to Eustace, replacing it with another cloth, freshly dipped in the ice-water.

There was the woman whom he had wished to marry—there was the mother who had given him life, and spent hers in ministering to his interest and comfort. Every other feeling faded before the image of that matchless mother, stretched out so helplessly on the bed, from which there seemed so small a hope that she would ever rise. Constance was only considered by him in the light of his mother's nurse—any middle-aged woman who contributed to Lady Yorke's comfort would have been equally valued by him.

Poor Constance had had many sleepless nights when he arrived, of which he knew nothing; but seeing how wearied he looked, she recommended his going to bed, and assured him she was quite fresh. He had travelled for three nights unceasingly, with the terrible dread lest he might be too late to see his mother; and the re-action of hope had upset the equilibrium of his mind; and, with his head buried in his mother's pillow, he had sobbed so helplessly, that Constance wept too from sympathy, but silently. She had been too much exhausted by continued watching to have much room for violent expressions of sorrow.

When Eustace awoke at the end of two hours, he came again to the sick-chamber, and found the patient was sleeping. A hurried sign from Constance made him stop on the threshold, to which she came on tiptoe. Preceding him into the ante-room, she wrote on a bit of paper,

"She has slept for an hour without muttering—it is the first good sign."

Constance had a wet handkerchief tied round her head—in no other way could she keep awake in the treacherous stillness of the sick-room. The water dropped on the paper, which called the attention of Eustace to the circumstance.

"I am quite refreshed now," he wrote; "let me take your place whilst she sleeps."

"I shall be glad to lie down for a little, if you will promise to call me when she stirs."

"I promise."

And Constance dragged her weary limbs to a sofa, and wrapping a large shawl round her, was asleep in half a second, lulled by fatigue and a slight hope that Lady Yorke might recover, after all.

CHAPTER VIII.

"Reviving sickness lifts her languid head—
Life flows afresh."
                                    THOMSON.

TWO hours subsequently Eustace called her—his mother had asked for barley-water—and Constance came in, gently, and without hurry, and directed Eustace in what manner he could lift the patient most easily, whilst she held the cup to her lips.

"That will do. Lay her down gently. So."

Lady Yorke turned her eyes languidly and saw her son. She evinced no surprise, but gave him a quiet smile of recognition, and closed her eyes again. The danger had abated, but any anxiety might reproduce it.

She was "very weak," the doctor said, and it would be very long, even did no relapse take place, before she regained her former state of health. This opinion Mr. Johnson expressed to Eustace, and was enthusiastic in his encomiums on Miss Rivers.

"It is a pity she should be a lady," he said, thoughtfully. "Nature intended her for a hospital nurse. I assure you, Sir Eustace, that the orders of a medical man are useless unless they are consistently carried out in his absence. I never saw any woman, even a professed nurse, so sleepless and untiring, so judicious, when compelled to exercise her own discretion—so tranquil, thus conveying tranquillity to the patient—so self-commanding, lest any emotions of terror or anxiety should affect the sick person. She has done much to save the life of Lady Yorke. You ought to be grateful to this young lady."

"I am, of course," said Eustace, in an indifferent tone. He was very grateful inwardly, but none like to be told what they ought to feel. "How long is Lady Yorke likely to remain in this state?" he inquired.

"That I cannot possibly say. A fortnight may see a great alteration for the better, or, if there be a relapse——"

"She will not have a relapse," said Eustace, impatiently. His brain had become irritable from anxiety and want of sleep.

"Well! well! we will *hope* not; but should such a contingency unfortunately occur, I think you must allow me to send a professional nurse to relieve Miss Rivers, whose health seems to me to be suffering from confinement and watching. That maid, Mrs. Watson, seems to me utterly useless in attending on her ladyship. She is always crying, which, if it evinces—which no doubt it does—great sensibility to the sufferings of her mistress, is a very inconvenient way of showing it."

"Indeed!" said Eustace, thoughtfully. "That must be looked to."

He did not desire to make Mr. Johnson *au fait* at all the little asperities of the subsoil of domestic life at Elm Hall. He remembered the vexed question of unbruised oats before he left home, on which occasion Kali Khan had complained of the disobedience of the groom to Eustace's orders; and he thought how often that faithful servant had hung about passages, and lurked in anterooms, to speak to Eustace since his return, never having found an opportunity, from the circumstance of Lady Yorke's danger.

"I must see Kali Khan to-day, and hear what this is all about, if I can leave the sick-room with any comfort to myself."

He went back on tiptoe, but Lady Yorke was awake; and Constance, very pale, but more lovely in the eyes of Eustace from that circumstance, arising, as it had done, from her devotion to his mother, was disentangling and brushing the patient's still beautiful and luxuriant hair. Eustace heard his mother speak feebly—

"Constance, you don't want to go home, do you?"

"Not till you are well enough to part with me with ease to yourself, dear lady."

"Oh! I don't know when that will be," said the invalid, wearily.

"Soon," replied Constance, trying to speak cheerfully, though her heart sunk at the idea of leaving Elm Hall. "Mr. Johnson says you will soon be well again, now the fever has subsided."

Lady Yorke was silent, and only answered by a slight pressure on Constance's slender hand.

"I shall have to leave Elm Hall, or break

my word to my mother," reflected Eustace. "I loved that girl at first sight; and seeing how admirable she is at the side of my mother's sick-bed has not disenchanted me. She seems all that a man could desire in a wife. I wonder if she could love me. My mother *must* consent—she *will*, willingly. I would not vex her, for the miseries of this illness has proved to me how far dearer she must ever be to me than any other woman. Oh! mother, cannot I love you both? How should such love be incompatible?"

But Eustace took care to avoid Constance as much as possible.

"I give you my word that I will not commit myself till I have your permission," had been his own words, and they were always ringing in his ears.

CHAPTER IX.

"Lives there a man who has not tried
How mirth can into folly glide,
And folly into sin?"

SCOTT.

IN the meantime, Lady Yorke, though recovering very slowly, was pronounced out of danger; and Eustace, thinking that discretion was the better part of valour, drove over to call on the ladies at Earlscliff, to find that safety in numbers which he had discovered to be so efficacious before the London season had commenced.

Before he left home he had a long and mysterious conversation with Kali Khan, the results of which did not transpire; but Mrs. Watson was observed to look more cheerful.

Surely the cloud of trouble had blown over.

After Eustace had been gone some hours, a mounted servant came with a note from Earlscliff, to say that he would not return to dinner, and had sent intelligence lest his mother should be anxious at his protracted stay. He returned about eleven o'clock, in cheerful spirits. The change had been pleasant to him after the depression and anxiety of the sick-room.

The next day he again rode over for a pic-nic—on the following to a croquet party. He had not explained to Lady Yorke why he left home so continuously, and she was far from giving him credit for his forbearance.

"Just like all young men," she thought —" one fancy succeeds another. That for Constance's beautiful face has been faded by the ladies of Earlscliff. Eustace, like the knight in the fairy tale, has fought with the dragon and wild beasts that stood in his career, but, unlike that hero, he seems bewildered by the lights, the perfumes, the flowers, and jewels of the enchanted hall. The dancing girls have entwined him in their wreaths of roses, and he who met danger with daring, is falling a victim to pleasure."

Eustace returned at night—sometimes about eleven, but frequently his stay was prolonged into the morning hours. Then Lady Yorke became anxious and sleepless. Constance had been too much accustomed to attendance on a beloved object both feeble and nervous, not to understand what she felt, even when she did not express her fears. Her ladyship was afraid of exciting her son's ridicule by confessing her terrors.

"If he would but take the close carriage, instead of driving that terrible horse without a servant, I should not mind so much," she thought.

Eustace knew that the old coachman was unused to go out at night, and utterly unfit at that period of the twenty-four hours to sit on the box, to say nothing of driving. He thought his mother almost absurd in her scruples about turning him away.

"A useless, debauched old man—better degrade him, and give him a small annuity, and send him away; but women, even the best of them, do not know how to manage men—they are too kind-hearted."

These were the reflections of Eustace, whilst every night Constance used to press her forehead against the dark pane in Lady Yorke's dressing-room, in order that her ear might catch the most distant sound of his horse's hoofs. Her ladyship knew of Constance's anxiety for her comfort, though the rich, heavy hangings of the bed, gathered at the foot-post, intervened between the patient and the open door which led to the ante-room.

"Are you afraid of cold, Constance?"

"By no means."

"Then open the window and lean out, and you will hear better."

"I think I hear the sound of wheels in the distance, but a great way off."

A long pause, during which Lady Yorke remained quite still, holding her breath, lest the slight rustle of the bed-clothes should interfere with the sounds of outward objects.

"Is it any nearer?"

"No," said Constance, rather ashamed; "I was mistaken, or the sounds have gone in another direction."

Constance hears a suppressed sigh from the bed; and, full of pity and tenderness, she strains her senses again in the hope of hearing better news to give next time. Then Lady Yorke, trying to be playful, would say,

"Sister Ann—Sister Ann, do you see anything coming?"

"I only see the trees waving, and the grass growing green," Constance would answer, from the nursery lore,

"Is it very dark?"

"Not very—I can see the edges of the clumps of trees against the sky."

"Is the sky cloudy?"

"It *is* rather, but Sir Eustace has lamps, my lady."

"How do you know?"

"I observed them when he drove off."

"I wonder if she is anxious about him also, for her own sake?" and in this meditation the mother half forgot her anxiety. Then there was a voice from the window.

"I think I see a light amongst the trees in the distance—no—'tis gone!" A silence.

"There it is again! It must be he!—it must be Sir Eustace!"

"Are you sure?"

"Quite sure. I hear the wheels now and the trot of the horse. He is coming down the drive of the avenue."

"Thank Heaven!" murmured the mother, with her face turned to her pillow.

In a few minutes Eustace came in, with his face still radiant with the cheerfulness of the circle he had left, and freshened by the night air. His first inquiry was directed to his mother, and then he turned to Miss Rivers to have the account confirmed, or neutralized, if he suspected Lady Yorke of stating what the prophet calls "smooth things"—deceits to make him easier about her health.

"Who gave you *that?*" said his mother one evening jealously, pointing to a rare exotic which adorned his button-hole.

"One of the girls," he said carelessly; "would you like to have it?"

And without waiting for an answer, he removed it from his coat and laid it on the bed.

"Thank you, my son."

She did not care for the flower, but she was pleased that he did not wish to retain it. He did not say much in answer to her questions about the party. He knew instinctively that she did not like the people with whom he had been spending the evening, and against whom he believed her to be unjustly prejudiced.

"I have given her my word—why cannot she trust me?"

Conscience told him that if he told her his happiness depended on his marrying one of those ladies, she was too fond of him to withhold her consent, even if she did not like his choice. He wished his mother would get well, and not compel him to "hold passion in a leash." How gladly would he pour out his whole soul to supplicate for Constance's love; but she was so shy—so self-constrained, that he was by no means sure of his ground with her—whenever they chanced to be alone she tried to get away. She was overwhelmed with shame at the recollection of the circumstances under which they had first met, and seemed fearful lest he should make any reference to them.

There was to be a large entertainment at Earlscliff—archery and croquet in the morning, and dancing in the evening. On that morning Lady Yorke was less well—suffering from restlessness, fever, and headache. She, however, declared that it was the result only of a sleepless night, and that she should be as well as usual on the following day.

"I wish I were not going," said Eustace.

"*Must* you go?"

"Yes—I ought. They have been very hospitable to me, and I know they are short of men. I must go, but I shall come home as early as I can."

"I wish you would stay the night there," said his mother, feebly. "It makes me so anxious your coming home alone—why not take Kali Khan?"

"Kali Khan, mother, is not fit for night air. The clime's too cold for him, meridian born, to bloom in. I should kill him in a week if I knocked him about in by-roads at two in the morning."

"Take John."

"Rather not, thank you, my mother. Pray don't worry, and remember it is a dance—I may be later than I wish to be. Good-bye," and he was gone.

Constance's occupation, when not reading

to Lady Yorke, was finishing a pair of slippers that lady had begun for Eustace, but her completion of which had been prevented by her illness. Whilst her ladyship slept, Constance was glad of the little interest of this light work. It was something to have an object to accomplish; but this was now at an end, and Constance rolled them up, and went out to stroll in the evening, feeling as depressed as did the worthy historian when he had completed "The Decline and Fall," &c., &c., and felt that his occupation, like Othello's, was gone.

CHAPTER X.

> " The sun went down in clouds, and seemed to mourn
> The sad necessity of his return:
> The hollow wind and melancholy rain
> Or did, or was imagined to complain:
> The tapers cast an unauspicious light—
> Stars there were none, and doubly dark the night."

THE sky was heavy and leaden in colour. The large masses of trees were motionless in the stagnant air, and the owl, with heavy wings, and long, tremulous cries, gave the only indications of life. August had arrived, but nature seemed to Constance to have a look portentous of decay. The reveries of the young girl were sad, and with reason. Her friend was less well. How human nature revolts from that word "worse!" "Not quite so well to-day," is the answer tenderly given, when "well" is the antipodes to the state of the patient.

Since the death of her foster-mother, Lady Yorke was the only female who had spoken kindly to, or looked kindly at her; and now she was threatened by her loss. Should her patient recover, she had no claims on Lady Yorke, nor could she expect to have the visit prolonged, which had been lengthened by accident to a preposterous period. She had written to her father to explain that illness of her hostess had delayed her return, and had had a business-like reply by the return of the post, saying:—

"Mark Lane, Friday, August 28th.

"Dear Constance,

"I have received your letter, and I think you are wise in staying so long as Lady Yorke finds you useful. Make my compliments to her ladyship, and I remain, yours affectionately,

"EDWARD RIVERS."

"Wise! As if my stay were for politic motives! He does not say he shall be glad to see me again. He does not even sign himself 'Your affectionate father!'" said Constance, bitterly.

She walked till the darkened sky began to distil large heavy drops of rain, and then she returned to the sick-room, where the housemaid was sitting in her absence; for Watson had been laid up for the last two days, from an attack similar, seemingly, to that of her mistress. Lady Yorke was lying quietly, and Constance dismissed the attendant, and walked to the window, leaning her forehead against the glass, outside which rain-drops with rugged sides were chasing each other down in quick succession. One side of the room commanded an old stone balustrade, and Constance looked out at the grey stones, between the crevices of which spiral grass had shot up, and gazed at the clusters of yellow mosses which had crept over its surface, and tried to calculate how long it would be before they would be united, and conceal the whole material. She took up a book, but the light was too faint to permit her to read, and though there was a light in the ante-room, she did not like to leave the sick lady to seek its proximity. It was a relief when the housemaid brought her a cup of tea and a plate of bread and butter, for Constance declined the formality of a dinner of which there was none but herself to partake. The French clock in the ante-room struck the hour of nine. Constance sighed as she thought how many hours must elapse before Sir Eustace returned.

"Pray, ma'am, do you think you will want me again to-night? I'll put the lemonade and barley-water for my lady."

"It is rather early—only nine o'clock."

"Yes, miss, but I've had a bad toothache all day, and——"

"Oh! go, by all means. You had better first give a look to Mrs. Watson."

"She've locked her door, miss, and I believe she's asleep."

"Good night, then," said Constance.

The maid's footsteps echoed along the old oak flooring of the passage, and it required all Constance's sympathy with a pain which she had only "heard of by the hearing of the ear," but, fortunately for her, had never suffered from, to prevent her following the servant to ask her to sleep in the ante-room. Whilst she hesitated the footsteps died in the distance, and the moment was past. Constance looked at the patient.

"How *very* quiet she is," she said, drawing her breath quickly, in vague terror. "Surely her face looks very grey," and she watched the slight movement of the bed-clothes over Lady Yorke's shoulder, that showed that, though feeble, the heart was not irregular in its action.

A little comforted, Constance seated herself by the bedside in an arm-chair. The rain seemed to be hurled against the windows by the violence of the wind which had arisen at nightfall, and clattered incessantly on the top of the large skylight which surmounted the Hall. The old oak panels seemed to groan and complain over some approaching misfortune to its owners. All kinds of mysterious noises echoed through the corridors. Constance was not a strong-minded woman. Images of her past life pursued her. The face of her dead foster-mother seemed palpable to her touch; more frightful scenes were re-enacted to her disturbed senses.

"Oh! that she would awake and speak to me!" said the poor girl; but Lady Yorke moved not, and spoke not. She became alarmed at what seemed to her to be not sleep, but insensibility.

CHAPTER XI.

> "I know not how it is,
> But a Foreboding presses on my heart
> At times, until I sicken. I have heard,
> And from men learned, that before the touch
> (The common, coarser touch) of Good or Ill,
> That oftentimes a subtle sense informs
> Some spirit of the approach of things to be."
>
> PROCTER.

SHE rang the bell repeatedly, but no one answered, the proper attendant having gone to bed with the toothache. At length the kitchen-maid came up, and when Constance explained that she wished the groom to ride directly to Dr. Johnson to beg him to come at once to see Lady Yorke, who, she was afraid, was worse—

"Lor! Miss, what a night! 'Tisn't a night to turn a dog out!"

"No, it is not. I would not turn a dog out, because it would be uselessly cruel, but I must turn out a man to deliver my message."

Thus adjured, the maid went out, and after the lapse of half an hour she returned, and said the groom was not in his bed, and she could not find him at the stables.

"'Tis most eleven," continued she in a consolatory manner; "and I daresay Sir Eustace won't be much after one, or two, before he's back."

She lingered a minute or two, and finding Constance made no response, withdrew. So Constance took her place again by the bedside, sitting bolt upright, half afraid of her friend's deep sleep, and more fearful lest the roaring of the wind, and the heavy splashes of water against the window, should awaken her, and render her more anxious than ever about the return of her son.

More and more nervous she grew as time went on. Eleven had chimed, then a weary hour. She listened to the death-watch which seemed close at her side, and which she had first mistaken for the ticking of Lady Yorke's watch, which she had in consequence removed into the ante-room, so irritable had her brain become from the constant recurrence of the small sound. The room was hung with dark tapestry, which in the violence of the tempest moved slightly from the eddies of wind behind it, giving a life-like swaying to some of the gaunt figures it represented. They appeared to be bowing to Constance with mocking courtesy. She tried to fix her attention on a well-executed branch of a gourd which seemed to fall over the side of a broken pillar, whilst the rich rounded fruit rested on the ground, and speculated whether she could imitate it in modern needle-work. Then she thought how many years since the fingers had perished which had executed this marvellous work—two hundred and fifty years at the least—and wondered if some former Lady Yorke had wiled away the hours of her lord's absence by this occupation, surrounded by her maidens, or whether the work had been done by the weary hands of manufacturers at Gobelins. The thought of the quick monotonous movements of their fingers made her drowsy, and she leant back in the chair and slumbered.

A low growl from a small lap-dog at the foot of Lady Yorke's bed startled her. She opened her eyes, too terrified to move, and gazed with distended lids at the object which she saw reflected from the ante-room in the cheval glass which stood in the bedroom.

A figure stood there, with the fixed pallid hue of a corpse—the blue lips were retracted from the clenched teeth, the hair fell in loose locks down the sides of the face, and partly over the shoulders, from which the white night-dress flowed below the feet. The look of horror in the face was unspeakable. Constance's lips formed the name of Watson, but her voice was unheard.

After a moment's pause, during which Constance fancied she heard the loud pulsations of her own heart, the figure advanced slowly, with the same fixed and stony aspect, and seizing Constance by the wrist, drew her away from the bed in the direction of the ante-room.

"She is mad. She will strangle me," thought Constance.

And she scarcely could repress a scream; but she followed without resistance, lest she should awake her patient, although Watson was not content with removing her from the immediate vicinity of Lady Yorke, and led, or rather dragged her along the corridor, and up the garret stair-case, till she reached the servant's suite of rooms, and had deposited her in her own.

When there, Watson seated herself on the bed, and burst into a fit of hysterical weeping, which comforted Constance, who thus imagined that, feeling herself worse, she had gone to her for company and succour.

"Sit down a moment," said the active young nurse. " I will get you some sal-volatile. She tried to leave the room, but Watson held her tightly by the wrist. " I *must* go back, and get you some medicine, Watson. Lady Yorke may awake. She will think me so unkind to have left her."

"You cannot go to her!" the woman gasped. " You must go elsewhere, or there will be *murder.*"

This announcement confirmed Constance

in the idea that Watson was mad, or delirious. She spoke a few soothing words, to which Watson paid no heed.

"You think me mad—I am not. Sir Eustace will be murdered to-night on his way home—and, oh!"—she gave a prolonged scream of horror and agony—"it's my own flesh and blood will have done it."

"Oh! Watson! don't say such dreadful things—it can't be! Who would murder Sir Eustace? He is good to everybody."

"Oh! miss! 'tis that black fellow always making mischief. First he made mischief telling Sir Eustace the corn wasn't ground for the horses; and then the false villain watched out of the little lattice window at the end of the house, that overlooks the stables, and he says he saw Jim carrying a sack of oats out, and giving them to another man to take away—robbing my lady,—and Sir Eustace declares he will prosecute Jim for the theft—and, oh!"—here the look of horror was intensified—"I overheard him tonight telling the man he gave the corn to that Sir Eustace should never persecute him, for he would *do* for him. And then they both went downstairs, and followed them, and they went into Sir Eustace's room. I stood back inside the little cupboard, where Jane keeps her carpet-brushes, and I saw Jim come out with Sir Eustace's revolver in his hand, and then I came to you."

"But how could you hear what they said?" inquired Constance, who was not certain, notwithstanding the reasonableness of the statement, that Watson might not be under a delusion.

Still holding her by the wrist, she led Constance into a large space intended for clothes.

This, which was rather a small room than a linen-closet, was next to the one in which the groom slept. Mrs. Watson pulled back part of a panel, and showed Constance how she had heard every word of the conversation, without being suspected by the groom.

"Oh! I've been miserable! I knew that poor boy had been led away to be up to mischief, so I listened."

"You must go at once and awaken the coachman, and send him to warn Sir Eustace."

"I can't—I can't!—poor father is never sensible-like this time of night!"

"The butler, or footman, then," said Constance, impatiently.

"Yes, and give my dear child to the gallows!—no, miss, I can't do that. A pretty thing to tell them that Jim was lurking to shoot his master!"

"But he ought to be punished, Watson, if he is so wicked."

"Oh!" said the woman, wringing her hands, "I *nursed* Sir Eustace, but Jim is my son—the child of shame!—my mistress don't know it. I called him my nevy—my sister's child, to her. No one knows but father. If you ever tell of me or of Jim, miss, I'll never live to have it cast up to me again!"

This conversation was carried on in whispers, interrupted by continued bursts of the tempest, which sounded even louder where they now stood, just under the roof.

"What do you wish me to do?" said Constance.

"You must go yourself to the cross-roads, and get Sir Eustace to come the long way. Jim, poor misguided boy, will wait in the oak piece."

"Could you not go yourself?" said Constance. "Sir Eustace will think it so odd; and how can I make him come home the *long* way in such a night as this, unless I tell him? *You* could tell him what you liked."

" I would go gladly, but I could not walk all that way—I should drop before I got to the end of the park. And, oh! miss, if Sir Eustace is shot, how will *she* feel?—and to know that you might have saved him!"

"You must stay with Lady Yorke—say I am sleepy, and gone to bed—say anything to keep her quiet—there is no time to be lost."

And Constance fastened a black kerchief over her head, knowing that her bonnet would not keep on; and put on a black paletot over her morning dress, so that no spot of white might draw attention to her, should anyone be out on so tempestuous a night.

CHAPTER XII.

> " Last night a gifted seer did view
> A wet shroud swathed round Lady gay—
> Then stay thee, fair! in Ravensheuch,
> Why cross the gloomy path to-day?"
> Scott.

LADY YORKE had been an active pedestrian before her illness; and Constance had walked with her all round the neighbourhood of the park, till she

> " Knew each copse and every alley green,
> Dingle and mossy dell, in that wild wood."

She knew the danger to herself as to insult and violence, even unto death, should she encounter either Jim or his ruffianly companion on her way to warn Sir Eustace. Unfortunately the direction to the cross-roads and that to the oak-piece were identical for a short way, and led through a thick plantation, at a considerable distance from the house.

"God grant she may be in time! Run, Miss, run!" was the parting injunction of Watson as she closed the back door softly on Constance, and then stole up to her lady's bedside.

When Constance found herself in darkness, her first impulse was to return and knock at the door, under which still came a glimmer of friendly light. The blast nearly swept her from her footing; the rain dashed in her face with a violence really blinding. She leant against the door, still too confused to remember in the intense darkness in what direction she was to advance.

"Eustace will be murdered if I do not proceed," she was ever repeating, as she stole along with arms outstretched, to save herself from contact with unknown objects. She must go the shortest way—yes, she knew that—by the cross cut through the park. Her thin-soled jean boots, which she had not had time to change, gave her notice when she stepped off the short sward which had been trodden by occasional passengers into some degree of solidity, and the soft deep turf into which she sometimes strayed.

She would come to the park palings soon —high, and covered with yellow lichen and creeping ivy. She must feel for a small gate to get outside the boundaries of Elm Hall. She could not find the latch which fastened the gate, and shook it in impotent irritation. What might not depend on haste?—and now her ignorance of this impediment, so simple in itself, might make her too late. She felt in the darkness, and tempest, and driving rain, which had drenched her to the skin, as if she were struggling in a nightmare, so impassable seemed this slight barrier to her further progress.

At length she passes her hand from the top to the bottom of the oak door, and her fingers encounter the latch. Thank heaven she is through!—but will she be too late? Even now she cannot walk very fast; the road is rough, and hurts her feet. She stumbles in her haste. Soon she will come to a wooden bridge—she hears the turmoil of the swollen waters already. As she gets nearer she sees flashes of light from the rush of the waves between the piles of the bridge. She must walk carefully now, and feel her way cautiously, if she is ever to reach the cross roads. She puts her foot on the plank—it is shaking, for the river is swollen by the rain, and involuntarily she withdraws it.

"Oh! mercy! mercy!—Father in Heaven, let me not perish yet!—not yet!" and she trod again on the bridge, which had no hand-rail, balancing herself with her arms, and placing one foot directly before the other, lest she should tread over the side.

It is past! What a blessing! She must try to run now—run as far as the wood, from which she will find a clear passage to lead her to the cross roads; but the wood is dark and entangled even in noon-day. How shall she find the path through it now? Her heart beats faster as she nears the mass of dense foliage, from which the leaves have not yet fallen this year, though the spoils of past autumns have encumbered the small path-ways.

On the outskirts there stood a low, mean-looking cottage, in the upper window of which a light was dimly burning. It looked like company, and she could not bear to leave its vicinity. She would knock and ask the labourer who lived there to walk with her to meet the dog-cart; she would promise him some money—10*s*. She had none in her pocket; she need not say why she went. It would not be like taking any of the Elm Hall servants. She knocked softly at first, but getting no answer, she knocked louder. After so long an interval that she was leaving the door in despair, she saw the light removed from the upper room, and in a minute a man with a shaggy head, and eyes half closed in sleep, demanded what she wanted. His appearance scared Constance so completely, that she thought she should dread such a companion more than solitude. However, she said, trembling, that she wanted to reach the cross roads—would he go with her, and show her the way through the wood?

"What d'e want to go there for?" was the not unnatural question of the man, who was as much disturbed at the apparition of Constance as she had been at his personal appearance.

Constance's countenance was white from terror, the drenching rain had beaten the scarf close to the sides of her face and throat, and her appearance was altogether woe-begone.

"'Tis the spirit of some woman who wanders about at night, that murdered herself, and is buried at the cross roads," thought the man.

"Pray, come with me," said Constance, gaining courage as the labourer seemed to hesitate. And she stepped forward on the threshold.

"Go away—don't touch me! I would 'na go with 'e for fifty pound—through that wood, too! Why, a man was murdered there nigh seven years agone."

He slammed the door, and Constance

turned away towards the fearful shadows of the forest, with a sinking heart. Her eyes had become accustomed to the darkness now, and she found her way to the path which led into its depths. When in the path, she was again compelled to use her hands and feet to help her perceptions of the locality. The wind whistled, and the dead branches snapped and hung above her head, swaying backwards and forwards for a few minutes, and then crashing to the wet ground.

Suddenly Constance stopped, and felt her lips turn icy cold with terror. She heard voices borne on the blast, and then dying away in silence. She remembered that Watson had said that the way to the oak pine and the cross roads led through the same wood. The two men were following her. Already she heard a nearer rustling of the branches and dead leaves close to her feet; the path diverged here—she felt hers was in one direction, and theirs, to the scene of their watching, was in another.

If they had not heard the rustling she made against the heavy branches, she might be unobserved; but should they find her, what reason could she give for being in that wild forest at night? They would guess she was going to warn Eustace, and kill her. How easily that could be done. Watson would never compromise her son by giving any clue to the subject, and Eustace would be murdered!

This pang was worse than all, for she loved him more than her own life. These thoughts flashed on her in an instant, and she stood still, lest she might draw attention by any movment. She heard the snuffing of some animal near to her. They must have a dog with them, and he was close upon her. With the agony of desperation she seized the branch of a tree, and swung herself up on it. She could not raise herself far—it was too dark; but she hoped the animal might not be able to reach her.

The crashing of the small branches which she displaced, followed by the quick barking of the dog, arrested the men.

"What's that?"

"Lord knows!"

And the one who first spoke suddenly turned the light of a dark lantern on the path.

Luckily the illumination fell on the lower part of the tree, to which Constance clung breathlessly, not venturing to move to a safer position, whilst the dog barked furiously round the trunk.

"Only a pheasant fell off its perch. No wonder, either, such a night as this. Come on, do!—we shall be too late—he will have passed the oak-piece, and then he will be safe, and we shall be *done*."

" I believe there's something in that tree," suggested the other. " The dog would never go on so for nothing."

"No use to wait," said the other, his teeth chattering with superstitious fear. " A man was found hanging there. A bit of business of Dick Hardress. Let's go on. I don't acre to stay too close to the place."

They called the dog angrily, and at length he left the tree to which Constance was clinging. She held her breath till the voices died away in the distance, and then dropped on the dead leaves, and urged her trembling feet in the opposite direction. She soon reached the open country—it should be a clover field, but she was not sure, till she had picked a bit of the trefoil, and felt for and counted the three leaves. There was a gate at the end of this field, and a well-marked hard path guided her to it.

"Now, if I am not too late, I shall save him!" she exclaimed.

The doubt was appalling; and Constance seated herself on the top of the gate, and strained her ears to listen, sick at heart at the dread that the horse's hoofs she heard might have passed where she was, and be carrying Eustace to destruction. No, blessed be the chance, the sound was drawing nearer!—she must prepare to arrest his progress. How could her weak voice be heard in the rushing of the wind? She must stand at the side of the road, at the risk of being knocked down.

"Sir Eustace!" she shrieked, "Eustace!—Eustace!—stop!"

He could not pull up at once, but he recognised the voice.

"Good heavens!—Miss Rivers!—my mother is worse?"

"Yes—no—oh! I don't know!"

"Can you get into the dog-cart by yourself? I dare not leave the reins to hand you in."

Constance climbed up, and the horse sprung forward after the momentary check.

"My mother?"

"She is asleep."

"Why, then, are you here?"

"Oh! you must turn back and go the other way!"

"Why must I?—for heaven's sake, do not interfere with the reins—the horse will not have it."

For Constance, in despair at finding they were both being carried along the road to the oak-piece, had put out her hand to turn the horse.

"Sir Eustace, you *must* turn back, and go the long way home!"

"I must have very good reasons given before I consent to that. Why, you are drenched to the skin, and trembling with cold! Constance, why did you come?"

"Oh! you must go back!—I implore you to do so, for the sake of Lady Yorke!"

"I must know why first."

"There are two men," she whispered, with her lips touching the ear of Eustace, "in the oak-piece, waiting to murder you!"

"Where did you get that bit of romance?"

"Never mind; but turn back. Oh!" she said trembling, "we are getting nearer to them every moment—*do* turn back!—have you no thought of *my* danger?" continued Constance, hoping thus to divert him from his purpose.

"This is nonsense," he said angrily; "you have much more chance of danger from cold by remaining in your wet clothes. We shall be home in ten minutes this way—the other is eight miles round."

Constance lost all hope; she looked at him, and saw that the only part of his dress which could attract attention was a comforter of white lamb's wool, which was twisted twice round his neck.

"I am so cold," she said; "I wish you would let me have that lamb's-wool scarf."

"Certainly—what a brute I was not to think of it sooner! Can you untie it yourself? I do not like giving Sultan a chance of doing mischief."

Constance withdrew the scarf, and passing it once round her neck, crossed the folds over her bosom. She knew what she did.

"No one cares for me—my life is valueless," she thought, "and I *may* save him!"

Then she closed her eyes, for she could see the oak-piece looming in the distance. She leaned her head against the shoulder of Eustace, with a vain hope of sheltering him. They were whirled along so rapidly, that she had half a thought that the ball might miss. She did not know the road rose in a steep acclivity, through woodland called the oak-piece, where the trees were surrounded by thick underwood, making a hiding-place nearly impenetrable to the eye even in broad daylight.

The moon shone out in fitful gleams as sombre masses of cloud swept hurriedly over her disc, and as the horse slackened his pace from the steepness of the rising ground, Eustace saw two dark figures steal from the side of the wood, the one in advance about to seize the reins, the other to come to the side of the carriage.

In an instant he saw that Constance's

terrors were well grounded, and that they were in an ambuscade—that the revolver had five barrels. There was a flash—then a report, another, followed by a moan. Sultan became unmanageable, and darted forward in a headlong gallop, which Eustace could not control, notwithstanding his frantic efforts to turn back and try to secure the murderers. Constance, too, lay a heavy weight on his left arm.

The horse, always inclined to be restive, was now startled into fury, which admitted but of guidance, and stopped only when he reached the principal entrance to Elm Hall, where Eustace generally alighted. Luckily, Watson, who had been listening with intense anxiety, came down and opened the door.

"Ring the bell, Watson, for Jim to take the dog-cart round, and then help me to lift Miss Rivers out of the cart—she is frightened, and has fainted, I fear."

Watson came out trembling, to receive the slight form of Constance, which Eustace deposited in her arms; but she nearly sunk under the weight.

"Confound that fellow! why don't he come?" said he impatiently.

Watson did not answer; she was dragging Constance out of the pouring rain into the hall.

Eustace thought the shortest course was to drive the horse round to the stable himself, and knock up the under-groom to attend to him. Then he strode back, worried and anxious, to the hall, and found Constance on the marble pavement, and Watson untying the lamb's-wool scarf.

"Do go up and see my lady, Sir Eustace; she is half crazy about your being out in such a night. She is making herself worse with her fidgets," said the waiting-woman; "and you must not say anything about

Miss Rivers—mistress believes she is in bed and asleep."

"I will speak to my mother, and then come back and carry Miss Rivers to her room," said Sir Eustace.

He went to Lady Yorke's bedside, and found her leaning on her arm, to catch the sound of the nearer approach of his footsteps.

"You are better, my mother? I'm quite safe, but very wet—'a damp stranger,' who will give you cold if he stays."

"God bless thee, my darling!" said the lady. "Sleep late to-morrow, or rather to-day, to recover your fatigue.

He kissed her brow tenderly, and left her, his mind anxious and distracted by Constance's fainting. She could not have been hit, surely? She had shrieked, but women always shriek at the sound of fire-arms!

He ran down the grand staircase, and came to the hall, where Watson was still supporting Constance on her knees—the white lamb's-wool scarf having been removed, had on the inside what seemed like crimson beads on its rough surface. Both Eustace and Watson gazed for an instant in horror.

"Where is she hit?"

"In the throat, sir, I fancy."

"Good heavens! 'tis my doing! I would not do what she entreated!"

. He said no more, but Watson knew what was meant.

"Light me. I will carry her up to her room."

Eustace stooped, and placed one arm under her knees, and the other round her neck; but she screamed at his touch, and he then passed his right arm under her shoulders, leaning her head on his breast. Thus they slowly ascended the grand staircase, till they turned into Constance's bedroom, where he laid her as gently as he could on the bed.

"Get off her wet clothes—I will ride directly for Mr. Johnson."

Constance opened her pain-expressive eyelids, and said faintly—

"Not you—send—promise—you owe me —something," she said, pointing feebly to the spot from which the blood was oozing.

Eustace chafed at the injunction.

"No one could ride as fast as I can— *pray* do not stop me!"

"You must not vex the poor young lady, sir—she's fainting again."

Constance made a feeble attempt to hold Eustace's sleeve, but her fingers unclasped.

"Please, sir, send the housekeeper to me —I shall want help."

Eustace said,

"Tell her, when she can understand, that I will not vex her by going myself—I'll send Jim."

Watson saw him leave the room with anxiety and impatience.

"I wish Mrs. Corrance would come. I must go, Miss Rivers. For the Lord's sake, look up!—if she isn't in a dead faint again! I can't help it—blood is thicker than water—I must see to my own."

She put her trembling hand into her pocket, and took out a small silk wadded case, from which she counted some notes, and sovereigns, and loose silver.

"It is not much, but he can't wait. It will be night before I can get the rest of it out of the savings' bank. Oh! will that woman never come? Where's the sal-volatile?—the smelling salts? What *can* I tell her about Miss Rivers?—better go and say she is not wanted, or it will all come out!"

She rushed out of the room, confident that Eustace would be too delicate to return whilst the women were supposed to be ministering to Constance, and went at once to Mrs. Corrance, whom she found in great tribulation, from the circumstance of having mislaid that part of her false hair called her front, without which she seemingly imagined she should be utterly useless.

"I wouldn't let Sir Eustace see me such a figure for all the world," she was saying to herself as Watson opened the door.

"You need not hurry. Miss Rivers was took in a kind of faint like, but she's all right now. You may go to bed again."

"Well, I shan't be sorry. To be sure, it flusters one so to be woke up, and the tiles have been rattling about so all night, and the wind a-roaring, and the rain splashing, as if the world was having a four weeks' wash."

So saying, she deposited the frontless head-dress, and re-donned the night-cap, preparatory to going to bed again. Watson took away her candle, to make sure of her not changing her mind, and went with tremulous and uncertain steps, as quickly as she could, to the rooms over the stables. There was a confused sound as she opened the door—an attempt at simulating the repose of sleep; but she had stepped lightly, and the preparations were ill carried out. She went at once to the bed, the clothes of which were drawn up over the person concealed beneath them; but Watson put her hand on the soaked hair and collar of the saturated velveteen jacket.

"I know all," she said, briefly. "You must fly, or be hanged for murder if you stay."

He glared at her with chattering teeth—his sin had found him out!

"Is he dead?" he said, in a low voice—
"I should not mind hanging for that."

"No, you cruel, godless wretch!—he has escaped. Oh! Jim, have you no feeling for me, who has brought you up from a babby, and been so good to you always, and loved you so?" and her voice went off in a sob.

He did not answer. He was revolving future schemes of vengeance, and Watson read this in his lowering animal brow, and sullen lips.

"You must go—oh! that *I* should say so!"

"Go? Yes. Where's a fellow to go without the brass? How's he to live, aunty?"

"There's all the money I have about me. Take the shepherd's pony. No, that will show which way you've gone. You must walk—run—to the station at Swindon, and catch the first train to London. Hide there till I can send you more money, and then go to Australia."

He rose sullenly.

"Needs must when the devil drives him," he grumbled.

"Kiss me, Jim, once."

"Don't come blubbering over a fellow so. I hate to have an old woman hanging over me."

"Write to T. W., at the post-office, to tell me where to send the money,—and now go."

"I'm shivered with cold—get me a bottle of brandy to take."

Watson went, and returned with a bottle of her mistress's best cogniac; and flinging her arms round his neck, she wept a parting blessing on his unworthy head, and saw him disappear out into the night. She watched to see that he had not encountered the undergroom, whom, when he found not Jim in his bed, Eustace had dispatched to find the doctor. Luckily for Eustace, Jim had not returned when Eustace went to the stable. He had just crept into it, when he was startled by his aunt's footsteps; who, having seen all that she was ever to see again of the creature she doted on, unworthy as as he was, returned to where she had left Constance, half insensible, and chilled by her wet clothes.

When Watson came to her bed, she gave no sign of life, except by repeated shudderings. Nurse cut her boots off, finding them too wet to be removed by any other means, and fetched hot bottles for her feet. She could not, however, without more aid, lift her to take off her wet clothes, which clung as closely as the boots.

"Miss Constance, you won't say anything about it, will you?" Constance did not seem to hear. "Miss Rivers, my dear, don't mention what I said."

Constance moaned.

"I don't think she can speak," Watson said, with a feeling of relief, "and I'll get Mrs. Corrance after all."

She did this, and Constance was undressed and comfortably laid in her bed before the surgeon arrived.

When he had examined the wound, which had bled afresh from the movement of undressing her, he found that a bullet had buried itself in her collar-bone. This he extracted, and set the bone which had been fractured by the concussion.

The shot had been made at too great a distance, luckily for Constance, to penetrate further, or she would not then have been alive. As it was, she showed no sign of consciousness, and her pulse was painfully feeble and indistinct. Sal-volatile was given her, and presently the pulse rallied, and Mr. Johnson left the room to give the intelligence to Eustace, who was restlessly walking up and down the dimly-lighted drawing-room.

An hour after, the doctor went to give, as he said, another look at the patient before he returned home. The inspection was unsatisfactory. Constance lay with her left arm bandaged close to her side, but the other was tossing wildly about the bed. Her cheeks were crimson, and her eyes sparkling with the unsteady light of delirium. Her mutterings were incessant. The words she uttered were incomprehensible by their being run one into another. Trouble, and terror, and great anxiety were conveyed in these shattered fragments of articulation, blunted as they were in their distinctness, and tossed together without proper sequence. Her pulse, though feeble, still was exceedingly rapid. Mr. Johnson looked grave.

"Probably anxiety has had something to

do with it, and cold. Did you say, Sir Eustace, that Miss Rivers was coming home in the dog-cart with you when she was fired at? Dear! dear! dear!—to take a lady out on such a night in an open carriage! Really, Sir Eustace, a leetle imprudent—eh?"

Eustace was provoked, and remained silent. He could not tell the surgeon that Constance had left the comfortable shelter of his mother's room to walk three miles through pouring rain to warn *him*, who would not take the warning, and who had probably sacrificed Constance to his own obstinacy. Mr. Johnson would go and tell his next patient that Miss Rivers, poor thing, was desperately in love with Sir Eustace, and they were about to be married forthwith, at least. Sir Eustace could scarcely do otherwise, under the circumstances.

Eustace could not fully understand why Constance had come, and on what information. One thing was certain—nothing could be said to her on the subject, till she was better, if that time should ever come. Eustace, though he loved Constance, and saw in this act a devotion to himself, most flattering to his self-love, would have given a great deal that it had not taken place. It mortified his pride that Constance should have been wounded for his sake, and that she should have placed herself in a false position in the eyes of the world, *i.e.*, in the small circle in which they lived.

Mr. Johnson was attending one of the ladies at Earlscliff, and would of course speak of the attempt on the life of Miss Rivers, narrating all the circumstances, and would hear from some of the party there that Miss Rivers had *not* been one of the guests at Earlscliff. However, Eustace was naturally taciturn, and left Mr. Johnson to his ignorance, trusting to chance to elucidate matters more satisfactorily than he could see any probability of at the present time.

CHAPTER XIII.

"Have you wit to be sensible of the delicacies of love? —the tenderness of a farewell, the sigh for the absence, the joy of the return, the zeal of a pressing hand, the sweetness of a little quarrel, caused and cured by the excess of love—in short, the pleasing disquietudes of the soul, always restless, and wandering up and down in a paradise of thought of its own making."

Love in a Nunnery.

"Nay, yet it chafes me that I could not bend
One will, nor tame and tutor with mine eye
That dull cold-blooded Cæsar. Prithee, friend,
Where is Mark Antony?"

TENNYSON.

EUSTACE did not like the chaff, so called by the vulgar, that would greet him at Earlscliff, the next time he went thither, from the '"bevy of fair women richly dressed," nor the congratulations on his safety, uttered with well-bred politeness and covered sarcasm, and the pitying and rather contemptuous inquiries after *poor* Miss Rivers, should all the story come out.

The lady of Earlscliff piqued herself on her power of attracting to her side all the *desirable* young or middle-aged men she met. She was youthful, and men said she was beautiful. The women pronounced her to be "quite plain;" but with dark blue laughing eyes, which could call up tears at a short notice, a harmless little nose, sweet small mouth, good complexion, like china, transparent with a bluish tinge, she found few who could resist her spells.

No man could boast of any greater favour from her ladyship than a kiss imprinted on the back of her small hand, yet she was as jealous of any real or fancied attachment to other women as if she had acquired the undoubted right to the allegiance of the eight or ten "friends" of her lord who visited at Earlscliff.

> " Favours to none, to all she smiles extends,
> Oft she rejects, but never once offends;
> Her lively looks a sprightly mind disclose,
> Quick as her eyes, and as unfixed as those."
> *Rape of the Lock.*

To women troubled by that irritable organ, the heart, Lady Levinge's line of conduct would have been dangerous; but though she must have possessed that seat of life, she did not metaphorically think she had one.

She had a good, quiet, serviceable tenderness for her husband and children, and strong ties of clanship to her own family; but though she delighted to believe that lovers were dying for her, and quite pitied what she called their "infatuation," the light-spirited lady entirely forgot their existence if they absented themselves a month.

> "Would Chloe know if you're alive or dead,
> She bids her footman put it in her head."

Eustace, with chivalrous devotion to her ladyship, would never profess more than she had a right to demand in her character of hostess, and in her "right divine" of youth, cleverness, and beauty. She was determined he should feel, and was always expecting the time to arrive when he should profess that "there was but one beloved face on earth, and that was shining on him."

"Whom do you love best in the world?" said the greedy fair, as they stood on a raised terrace overlooking from some distance a level lawn, on which a party were playing croquet.

"Do you really wish to know?" said Eustace, with a certain amount of fun scintillating in his blue eyes; but they were turned away, and Lady Levinge did not see the mirthful glance.

"Yes, you *must* tell me at once," and she looked aside, expecting tremulous tones and a tender gaze, and a pressure from his hands.

"My mother," said he bluntly; "I have never seen any woman to be compared with her."

"Ah!" said the lady in a tone of pique, "*that* is quite a different thing!" and, with a flush of anger and disappointment, she walked towards the party of croquet-players.

The rosy wreaths were already entangling the arms of the young warrior, and it was the silvery tones of Lady Levinge's voice, in observation on poor Constance's adventure, that he dreaded so much. True, Constance had probably saved his life, and certainly risked, if not lost, her own in the effort; but I doubt whether any man was ever grateful to a woman for saving his life, under any circumstances, even of the utmost devotion.

As he meditated on this subject, Mr. Johnson produced the bullet which he had extracted from Constance's collar-bone. Eustace took it mechanically, with wandering thoughts, but was arrested by astonishment. Conviction rushed through his brain in a moment. The bullet was one of several he had cast himself, and which he recognised from a little mark, not amounting to a defect, in its formation, observed when he was loading his revolver.

He left the room immediately, to see if the revolver was over the chimney, where he had left it. It was gone. Then the shot had been fired by one of the household, who had taken the fire-arm for the purpose of shooting him. Who had any reason to hate him? He knew of the robbery, and had threatened to prosecute Jim, and had delayed only till Lady Yorke could be consulted, as he did not like to resort to ulterior measures with regard to her servant without her sanction. He had contented himself by having locks placed on the corn-bins, the keys of which were held by Kali Khan.

Eustace returned to the breakfast-room, without saying anything of his suspicions to Mr. Johnson; and, by remaining standing whilst he lingered, at length got rid of that talkative gentleman, who, with many others of his tribe, seemed to love to remain as long as possible in the dwellings of the great, whilst he economised his time to the fraction of a minute in the hovels of the poor.

Eustace first paid a visit to his mother, and gave the morning salutation, which she always expected, and rejoiced in her amendment—the deep sleep, which had scared Constance by its semblance to death, had been the agent of life, and she seemed on the high road to convalescence.

"I wonder Constance has not been here yet," she said thoughtfully; "she is generally here at seven in the morning."

Eustace replied that he understood from the servants that Miss Rivers had a bad cold, and was not well enough to rise.

"Let Johnson see her," she said anxiously; "he may not be gone. I would not have her ill on any account—she is so very charming to me."

Eustace smiled sadly.

"Is she not?" her ladyship inquired.

"You *know* my feelings towards Miss Rivers, my mother. I have not ventured to express them to her yet, in deference to your wishes."

"Ah! Eustace, when I stood in the valley of the shadow of death, I felt what an inestimable comfort were the kind young hands that ministered to me—the kind soft voice that whispered comfort—the strong arms that turned me on my weary bed; and I thought, shall a selfish desire to monopolize my son's love deprive him of those consolations which the closing hours of life demand, and which must be sown in youth if they are to bear fruit in age. Constance seems to me to be sweet-tempered, intelligent, and ladylike; and, moreover, she sings charmingly, for one utterly untaught, though she cannot delight you with your favourite sonatas."

Eustace listened vacantly, if not impatiently. His mother had grasped his hand with her attenuated fingers, and he was thinking how to disengage them; the hope of winning Constance for his bride was second to his burning desire to search for some clue to the discovery of the murderers. Constance, tossing in delirium, with a fractured collar-bone, and a serious wound in her throat, cried for vengeance in his imagination—a desire increased by the notion of the domestic treachery revealed by the absence of his revolver.

He went to the stables, and found that James Watson was absent—no one had seen him go out, nor knew when he might be expected. Eustace then walked to the scene of the attempted assassination of the previous night.

CHAPTER XIV.

"The morn is up again, the dewy morn,
With breath all incense and with cheeks all bloom;
Laughing the clouds away in playful scorn,
And living as if earth contained no tomb."

THE sun shone out after the tempest which had swept over the face of Nature, who, like a capricious beauty, seemed to try to obliterate the remembrance of past violence in her present suavity. A soft steam rose from the ground, overcharged with wet, under the influence of a warm autumn sun, which sparkled in the dew-drops, caught like innumerable diamonds in the tangled lines of broken cobwebs, suspended from branch to branch of the blackberry stems, already turning in their crimson to purple fruit; the long grass was bent and soaked by the wet; but the shining leaves of the briony, confident in its support from the stiff sticks of underwood round which it clung, had gained fresh beauty to its scarlet berries and shapely-cut foliage, through which it glistened.

> " So fair the scene so formed for joy,
> So cursed the demons that destroy,"

said Eustace, as he passed along at a quick pace, contrasting it in his mind with the deed perpetrated on the previous night. When he came to the oak-piece, he saw distinctly the footsteps stamped into the wet ground, where the men had stood when waiting for his approach, and where their steps diverged, as one went in advance of the horse, and the other to the side of the carriage. From the hurry in which the latter had fired, the first had not had time to seize the rein, and the start made by the horse, at the report of the revolver, had precipitated the animal out of reach of his assailant.

They seem to have stood a moment looking after the cart, judging from the footprints, and then returned in different directions to the underwood for the purpose of escaping. One had worn hob-nailed-shoes —he who had attempted to seize the rein— but it was about the other Eustace was most interested. He observed them narrowly; fitted his own boot to each, and found them fill exactly the impression made by the assassin.

It was conviction to his mind, for he had a short time previously given a pair of his own boots to Jim. He followed the traces to the side of the wood—saw where the man had sprung into it, from the broken shrubs and bended grasses. He would probably have secreted the revolver somewhere in the neighbourhood. The wet leaves of last autumn, and the elastic moss, retained no marks of footsteps. He calculated that the revolver would not have been concealed under dead foliage only, which the whirling wind might at any time, by displacing, reveal; so he walked along by the side of the ditch, looking alternately at the weeds and short shrubs which rose a few feet above its depths.

Lady Yorke used to say that Eustace should have been the son of a North American Indian, from his shrewd attention to trifles, and from the sound reasoning he deduced from them. When five years old, his mother told him to go to the nursery and inquire whether a large unframed picture had fallen from the wall against which it had been hung, or if it had been taken down. He returned immediately and said,

" It has fallen down. There is no one in the nursury—I see nurse in the garden."

" How do you know?"

" Because," said the child, " it rests on the little edge of wood just above the ground. No one would have put it there, so it must have fallen."

It was, therefore, an enjoyment as well as an interest to Eustace to track the murderer; and had he found the revolver lying in his path, I doubt whether he might not have been exceedingly disappointed.

At length he came to a spot where the web-like tracery of the clover and the lilac plumes of the feathery grass, fully seeding, were interrupted in their continuity. He looked more closely, and saw the broken leader of a seedling oak, showing its white wood fractured, through the bark stripped down by some superincumbent weight. He put his hand and arm down to the bottom of the water which partly filled the ditch, and drew from it his revolver.

He would have justice on these scoundrels, was his first thought—he would send the detectives on their track. No regard to the feelings of Watson should interfere with his just vengeance. What would his mother think? Would she shield Jim for the sake of her maid? He thought not. Such a feeling must not be recognised if she did. He must act for himself in this matter, and instead of returning to Elm Hall, he walked in the direction of the county town, to take steps to pursue the criminals.

As he proceeded, he was more and more puzzled to know how Constance had discovered their design. The poor girl could give no account of the transaction in the disturbed state of her brain, which reflected only images broken and blurred. He was glad when he had accomplished his object, and turned his steps towards home. His mother could not long be kept in ignorance of what had happened, and it was desirable that she should know the circumstances so soon as she was capable of hearing them without injury to herself.

It had been well had Lady Yorke been sooner told. When Eustace arrived at home he proceeded to her room, but found her bed empty; and on going at once to the door of Constance's chamber, which was half opened, he saw his mother standing in her dressing-gown by Constance's bed, whose voice, in a sharp, unnatural key, rang through the darkened room in terrible contrast to the stealthy steps of the attendants, and their efforts to preserve silence.

" They are coming—coming!—the dog!— he'll catch me, and hold me for them ! Murder!—murder!" she shrieked; " they have tied me down not to warn him !" and she strove madly to undo the bandages that confined her left arm.

One of the servants held her right hand forcibly.

"You must not, Miss Rivers—you must not, indeed."

Lady Yorke observed the marks of blood oozing through the linen which covered Constance's throat, and turning, saw Eustace in the ante-room, and hurried to obtain an explanation from him. When he had told all he knew, and Lady Yorke, though unaccustomed to tears, had shed them abundantly at the recital, both mother and son proceeded to Watson's bed-room, to see what she knew of last night's proceedings. The maid argued in her own mind that she might as well make a clean breast of the whole affair, excepting her knowledge of Jim's hiding-place, shrewdly guessing that her effort to save Eustace, by sending

Constance to warn him, would propitiate Lady Yorke; and being moreover pretty certain that Jim, with the command of money which she had given him, would be certain to conceal himself in London till she sent him enough to obtain his passage to Australia. She hoped he would go there. All her love for him did not carry her to the point of wishing him to remain in England, where his evil doings were a constant source of anxiety to her. So she confessed all about him, excepting the tender tie which bound him to her. This must be concealed to the last, for Lady Yorke had no sympathy for those who climbed over hedges to pluck forbidden fruit; never having felt temptation herself, she had no sympathy for its results in others.

They left her with kind words. They pitied her for her relationship with a creature so unworthy as her nephew; they assured her that the shadow of his misdeeds should never be cast on her, if they could prevent it; but they made no promise to relax the pursuit of the offenders, and Watson did not ask what she felt could not be granted.

Days passed on slowly and sadly at Elm Hall. Constance's mind still wandered over the terrible circumstances of her midnight journey. Lady Yorke nursed her tenderly, and Eustace, with his reading or writing in the ante-room, was close at hand to hope or fear with every change in her malady. At length the delirium came on only at night; the morning hours had some portion of sound sleep, and a tint of health began to replace the painful hectic flush that had burned on her attenuated cheeks.

In the meantime, Lady Levinge pined for the toy which she could not obtain. Eustace had never returned to Earlscliff after the night of the storm, and all kinds of contradictory rumours were afloat with regard to the circumstances which had then taken place. Mr. Johnson had in attending his patient at Earlscliff been exceedingly mysterious in his half-communications—" Could not stay a moment longer—must ride as fast as his horse could carry him to Elm Hall—most interesting case—sweet young creature—great danger—Lady Yorke in the greatest distress—Sir Eustace almost distracted."

All this he said, and nothing further would he communicate—like an accomplished coquette, who, playing with her fan, reveals and conceals by fits and starts fragments of the story conveyed on it.

These broken bits of intelligence drove her ladyship nearly distracted with curiosity, and what she began to suspect was—love.

"No—can it be?" she asked herself,

"that I, who never cared for very much in the world excepting my own comforts, should have begun to be really unhappy because one insensible young man does not fall down and worship my pretty little person, enshrined in Earlscliff? This is nonsense—I'll think no more about him, but take a stroll down the Pleasaunce with Captain Lymerton."

In the most bewitching of hats—a wideawake of grey felt, bound by a blue silk kerchief, and a black mantilla thrown over a light muslin dress, Lady Levinge trailed her delicate draperies over gravel and turf, attended by the favoured youth, whose face beamed at the unusual honour. But a man may be what is now called "spoony," and be only more awkward and stupid in consequence thereof.

Captain Lymerton was a cavalry officer, and a fair amateur steeple-chase rider; but his attractions to the fair sex consisted in a handsome person, and a manner which would have been gentlemanlike but for its conceit. After he had implied that he thought Lady Levinge looked more than usually lovely that morning, and that her hat was charming, he had no more to say.

"Oh! that I had been created a man," thought the fair dame; "how *I* should have made love!"

However, she always abided by a rule to make others as happy as possible, so she led him to talk of horses, and he grew communicative in describing the merits of his two brood mares and their foals, and prophesying what wonders they were to accomplish in future seasons. From his mares he became discursive to his hunters, and began to boast of the way in which they carried him *first* in the field.

With the natural desire women feel to hear the men they love spoken of, Lady Levinge asked, "if Sir Eustace was not a very forward rider?"

"Yorke? Aw!—well, yes. He rides fairly—pretty well!"

Of Eustace's riding, excepting at the first burst, Captain Lymerton never had had an opportunity of judging; and even then the back seams of his red coat were all the gallant youth could have an opportunity of observing; but he became jealous the moment Lady Levinge had mentioned the name of Eustace, and determined to run him down to her ladyship.

"Sir Richard," replied her ladyship, "says that Sir Eustace rides very 'forward.'"

"Sir Richard is *so* good-natured," rejoined the young man, anxious to inflict uneasiness by a sneer, to make up for that which he had himself felt.

Her ladyship felt the sarcasm, and for the moment she hated her companion. When fair creatures let their little feet stray, even for an instant, beyond the straight gravel path of the proprieties, they must expect a sting from some noxious insect concealed in the soft herbage; but a woman is seldom at a loss for some weapon of offence, snatched from the armoury of her wit. Seeming to conceal a half yawn with her embroidered pocket-handkerchief, she replied in a listless tone,

"Ah! it is a perfect wonder to me how he can contrive to endure the set of stupid men with whom I surround him—men whose acquirements are inferior to those of the North American Indians; for these can neither ride, shoot, nor speak the truth; and though they pretend to the two first accomplishments, they are generally found deficient when put to the test."

Captain Lymerton winced. Lady Levinge, not content, thought she would follow up her advantage.

"I do not, however, include Sir Eustace in this category; to his other perfections, too, he may boast of this—that he never speaks a word to the disadvantage of the absent, nor denies them their fair share of commendation."

"Aw! yes—very true; he's a good fellow," said the Captain; "and I hope he will be happy, I am sure, in the state of life into which it has pleased fate to call him— as I used to say in my Catechism when I was a good little boy."

"What do you mean?"

"Is it possible Sir Eustace has not mentioned the beautiful girl who is staying with Lady Yorke, to whom the old lady is about to marry him, they say?"

"Ah! yes, I know," said her ladyship,

who felt a sudden spasm at the heart at this unlooked-for intelligence, which elucidated all that had seemed incomprehensible in the conduct of her hero. " I know all about it ;" and, to conceal the sudden pallor which blanched her face, she stooped over a low rose-bush, and tried to detach a bud from the stem. She twisted the bark, but it was tough, and would not give way; she wounded her fingers with the thorns, and bruised the delicate petals by the violence with which she plucked at the flower. " Pshaw!" she said angrily, " 'tis not worth the trouble," and she left it swinging on the tree.

" Certainly not worth the trouble," said Captain Lymerton, deliberately ; " few things are worth any. I am sorry you are so wounded," continued he, maliciously, but looking at a small crimson spot on her handkerchief, proceeding from the puncture of the thorn.

Lady Levinge was wounded mentally more than bodily. She walked onward with a fixed smile on her face; she was not aware that she was gazing on the objects which filled the Pleasaunce—the tall, clipped yew hedges, the stone statues of Prince Rupert and Prince Eugene, in their proper costume, and the other eight statues of Grecian deities, without any costume to speak of at all; the branches of climbing roses, which ran up on smooth green leafless stems within the yew fences, and surrounded them with a brilliant coronal of colour and atmosphere of perfume. Her senses took in all around her unconsciously—it was photographed, as it were, into a background to her present train of thoughts, and returned involuntarily in the solitude of her boudoir, and in the darkness of midnight. Worse than all was the "conviction" it gave her of the state of her own feelings. Such agony could only result from a deep absorbing passion for a young man whom she could not reproach with a single word or look which Sir Richard might not have heard or seen.

"I am astonished," she said, turning to her companion, "that the information which Sir Eustace communicated to me confidentially should have already reached you."

"*I* did not hear it from Sir Eustace Yorke," replied Captain Lymerton; "*we* are not on confidential terms. You know, I imagine, also, the romantic adventures which took place the other night. If they have not been communicated to you confidentially —perhaps you will aid me to piece the shattered fragments of information I have received."

Lady Levinge felt her interest overpowering her prudence.

"I have not seen Sir Eustace," she said,

"since our party. What have you heard?"

"Oh! my news did not come from a very aristocratic source, though perfectly 'reliable,' as the newspapers say. My groom had some conversation with that solemn creature who drives the apothecary, as to whether hot or cold applications were most efficacious in reducing inflammation in the hoof, arising from the prick of a nail. Probably he thought a doctor's servant would be better informed on such a subject than those who serve a stupid or less-gifted master. After fomentations had been discussed, the doctor's man said there had been an attempt to murder Sir Eustace on his return from Earlscliff, and that a young lady had thrown herself in the way and received the bullet intended for her lover—quite affecting, I declare! He added that there was still hope of her recovery; and asked whether the young lady was as beautiful as folks said, as he supposed she had been here at the party. He had never seen her himself, as she was always in Lady Yorke's room when his master was at Elm Hall. Are you ill, Lady Levinge?" for her ladyship hung suddenly on his arm with a little cry.

"No—nothing. I twisted my ankle a little—it will go off in a minute or two."

Captain Lymerton was unconscious whether it was real or pretended pain that had extorted the exclamation; but he was grieved for her suffering, now he had been revenged himself for the slight she had put on him, and entreated her to lean all her weight on him.

"Would you permit me to carry you to that seat?" he said, pointing to one placed in the recesses of the yew hedge.

"I can walk, with your assistance, thank you," said the lady. When she had reached the seat, she said, "I am very troublesome, but if you would not mind returning to the house, and sending my maid to me with a broad ribbon, to bind over my instep, I should be so very much obliged."

"I will fly," said the Captain; "but can I leave you alone? You look so very pale."

"Pray go at once."

And he went.

CHAPTER XV.

"Your affections are
A sick man's appetite, who desires most that
Which would increase his evil."

SHAKSPEARE.

"THANK heaven he is gone! Let me try now to think. I cannot remain in this suspense. I must find out the truth of this unintelligible story. I must get back to the house, and shut myself in my own room. I fear that he suspects that I love Eustace. What madness! I never knew that I did so myself till this morning. Let me get away, they will be coming after me directly."

And she felt like a hunted animal, and stole away through one of the openings in the Pleasaunce, into some high tangled grass, through which, by a circuitous route, she could reach the back of the house and steal up into her room.

Thither she ordered her luncheon to be brought. Like the Julie of Rousseau, she was *un peu gourmette,* and enjoyed the pleasures of the palate. Resembling also a more regal personage, Anne Hyde, who, when she used to hear of any fresh act of inconstancy on the part of the Duke of York, sighed—

" Alas! then cut me the other wing off the chicken!"

When she had eaten a cutlet, and drunk a glass of sherry in the seclusion of her sitting-room, she felt comforted, and better able to carry on the war. First she sent a pretty message to Sir Richard, that she should like to drive out with him after luncheon; and when that unsuspicious and honest gentleman gave assent, and felt delighted at the proposition, she assured him that she had been very remiss in never having called to inquire after the health of Lady Yorke during her dangerous illness, and expressed a wish, to which he agreed at once, to proceed to Elm Hall for that purpose.

CHAPTER XVI.

"A charm may peep, a hue may gleam,
But leave the rest to fancy's dream."

Anacreon.

THE day was sultry, and the flies troublesome to the pretty delicate white ponies which her ladyship drove. The lady was thoughtful, but sweet-tempered. Sir Richard was sufficiently occupied by looking at his neighbours' crops, and observing where the fields were cleared, and what land was bushed for the benefit of the sportsman and the perplexity of the poacher.

When they reached the lodge gate of Elm Hall, a fly from the neighbouring station was standing outside, and a brisk dialogue was going on between the lodge-keeper and the occupant of the back carriage. To this Sir Richard and Lady Levinge listened with much edification, and more amusement.

"For, love 'ee! de mean to say I mawn't ride up?"

"I'm very sorry, ma'am, but 'tis quite against orders. Much as my place is worth whilst the young lady is so ill."

"I shouldn't make much noise."

"'Tis the noise of the wheels on the gravel, you see, ma'am."

"I 'ed best walk up, p'raps; but there's the portmanty—the ban'-box I could carry."

"No doubt, ma'am, if you are *expected* at the house, one of the under-gardeners will come down for your luggage."

"Well, for the matter of that, I can't say they look for me; but when I heard that sweet young cretur' was like to die—hi, coachman! Take this pormanty down, and take it inside this good woman's cottage."

The "portmanty" was an imitation leather trunk, bound with lines of scarlet leather, and ornamented with the liveliest and biggest of brass nails. The man obeyed, and opened the door of the fly for the occupant to alight. At the moment she was about to do so, the horse, made fidgety by the flies, and by the prancing of Lady Levinge's ponies behind him, darted forward, and Mrs. Mag, resplendent in a silk dress, fully flounced, and diversified by broad stripes of blue and yellow, with a crinoline of majestic circumference, fell forward on her hands and knees on the hard gravelled road.

When ladies put on crinolines, they should allow their imaginations to rove beyond the bound of probabilities to those of possibilities.. Little did Mrs. Mag, not being a person of any play of imagination, fancy, when she put on that excellent contrivance for giving grace and dignity "to that important charge, the petticoat," the ridiculous figure she appeared, when, by the pressure of her person on the front of the hoop, it stood out in a bold circle in the opposite direction——but these are circumstances and situations in which the faithful historian is compelled to pass over the page with a pen undipped in ink.

Sir Richard sprung out of the pony-chaise to lift up the discomfited lady. Lady Levinge turned her head away, and covered her face with her handkerchief. Hearing footsteps, Mrs. Mag turned round a rueful face when rising, but seeing Sir Richard's sympathising countenance, she said with a groan,

"Lift me up, good gentleman, for mercy's sake!"

Sir Richard was not a tall man, though sufficiently strong and firmly set, but it took all his strength to lift Mrs. Mag up on her legs.

She had no sooner recovered her equilibrium, than she nearly lost it again; for, with this pithy observation, " ease before manners," she raised up her dress, and regarded, with an inclination to cry, a pair of very fat knees, denuded of the stockings, which hung down over the low garters, and indented and bleeding from the gravel which had wounded their fair circumference.

" You had best go into the lodge and get the woman to bring some warm water —that is what I should do if my favourite mare had cut her knees," suggested Sir Richard.

This gentleman was an excellent amateur actor of low comedy, and celebrated for his impersonation of old women. He was taking notes mentally, whilst Coralie, occupied with her ponies and her sad thoughts, had yet time to congratulate herself on the vulgarity of her rival's friends.

The lodge-keeper retired inside to warm some water, and Mrs. Mag seated herself gingerly on her "portmanty," striking out her legs, which she could not bend without pain, and revealing a very solid pair, terminated by a pair of smart lilac boots, so tight as to make the leg bulge over them.

"To think," said she, "that all this comes of my being good-natured! Good gentleman, just hand me that basket I brought with me."

She took from it a bottle of sherry and a wine-glass.

"Luckily I brought it! Your good 'ealth, sir, and your good lady's there," and having tossed it off, she declared that she was better now, having been "all of a twitter" before. She then wiped the glass with her handkerchief, and filling it again, pressed it on Sir Richard. "Let's be comfortable," said she, with a broad smile expanding over her benevolent face.

Sir Richard said that he regretted he could not pledge her, having taken luncheon so recently; and was amused with the thought how unspeakably absurd he must look hobnobbing with this extraordinary figure seated on her "portmanty," her hand balancing her wine, looking like an overgrown Bacchus, no longer fair and young, on his cask. The vine which clustered over the lodge made a suitable background to the subject. When Sir Richard had replenished her wine-glass, Mrs. Mag's tongue became lively, and she began to give him various bits of information as to her domestic arrangements.

"You see, sir, Betsy as is my cook at the willy, her half-sister live here as kitchen-maid to my Lady Yorke—ah! *she's* a nice lady as ever I see—so, says I, 'Betsy, when you write to the Hall, just ask how Miss Rivers and my lady get on together, for she's a sweet creeter; and if she felt uncomfortable like she should come and stay at the willy all the rest of her life, if she would; and then if she and Theo should fancy one another, Mr. Mag would do something 'andsome for his only son'—so, says I, 'you write, Betsy. Lor! edication is so wonderful now-a-days!—would you believe it, sir, more letters come to the maids nor they do to me! Well, you see, I love the poor gal—she've got no one at home; for Betsy—that's Betsy Rivers, not my Betsy, she've got a temper of her own. Step-mothers hate step-daughters; so Betsy's half-sister—that's Betsy, my cook—she wrote back—

Mary is *her* name—says she, 'Miss Rivers is not expected to live, for she's got shot somehow by the groom, and nobody can say how it happened.' But, do you know, Betsy says, sir—" and Mrs. Mag's voice became low and sepulchral in a stage whisper —" they say that she run three miles in nothing but her chemise and flannel petticoat, and nothing but her slippers on!"

"Who ran—Betsy?" inquired Sir Richard.

" No, sir, Miss Rivers, and 'twas a-pouring rain, and she got drenched. What must her feelings have been, poor gal!"

" And whither did she go?" inquired Sir Richard, whilst Lady Levinge listened curiously.

" Why, to Sir Eustace."

" Bless me! what an extraordinary story! What must his feelings have been to find a young lady running after him in such a very —very—well, we will call it a very unusual *demi-toilette.* Pray, ma'am, how did Sir Eustace behave under such very trying circumstances?"

" Why, he took off his coat, and wraps—and——"

" What, ma'am?—what other article did you say?"

" No, sir—not as I heard on; but you're trying to make game of me, and I don't deserve it at your hands; though you did lift me up, I'm not to be put down by you and your lady there, and her wicked eyes is a-dancing over her pocket-handkerchief, as if they was full of laughing tears. But I'll not be beholden for your company any more, sir!"

Just then the woman came from the lodge to say that the water was hot, and Mrs. Mag tottered in, holding by the doorpost, and muttering angry observations on Sir Richard and his wife. The fly-man, who had drawn up his horse at a little distance, came up and asked if he was to wait, and drive the lady back, or would she pay him? Mrs. Mag, feeling that she could not possibly walk up to the Hall, and as the woman was determined she should not drive up, resolved to go back to the Railway Hotel and write to Lady Yorke, to offer to come and nurse Miss Rivers.

Sir Richard, after leaving his own card, and that of Lady Levinge, to be forwarded to the Hall as soon as possible, drove off with his wife, with a countenance brimming over with merriment; whilst Coralie was divided between her malicious satisfaction at the seeming *entourage* of her rival, and mortification that a girl with such vulgar associates could ever have attracted a man so refined as Sir Eustace Yorke.

CHAPTER XVII.

> " The whispered tale
> That, like the fabling Nile, no fountain knows,
> Fair-faced deceit, whose wily, conscious eye
> Ne'er looks direct. The tongue that licks the dust,
> But when it safely dares, as prompt to sting."
> THOMSON.

IT was the custom at Earlscliff when, at eleven or half-past, according as my lady was in the mood, the female guests retired to their sleeping apartments, that the gentlemen should congregate in a room set apart for smoking at night, and for receiving any one who came during the day on magisterial or farming business. Here, in the repose of Sir Richard's sanctum, his guests discussed such of the ladies with whom they had passed the evening, as were fair game from being unfenced by the ties of consanguinity or marriage with any gentleman present. Here the rein was given to all the pent-up fun and *double entendre* which had been sealed within their lips in the company they had left. No doubt the ladies, too, in loosened corsets, flowing dressing-gowns, and unbound tresses, when they gathered together, as preference led them, in the sleeping-rooms of their particular friends, made themselves merry, as was their wont, on the many weaknesses and absurdities of their masculine acquaintance.

As Lady Levinge generally piqued herself on the beauty and attraction of her guests, and avoided as much as possible the chaperonship of mothers and aunts, the ladies, with their soft skins and shiny hair, which grew more and more sleek under the sleepy brushing of their maids—with the rich background of damask hangings, the soft lounge chairs, pensile lights in chased silver sconces, and an atmosphere of perfumes round them, would have been a more attractive spectacle than the gentlemen seen dimly through a cloud of tobacco smoke.

On the evening in question the curious spectator would have seen more, for Sir Richard, padded to a redundant circumference, and dressed in a costume borrowed from the cook, with a light "front," and a gay bonnet placed at the back of his head, and a tremendously smart silk dress, was seated on a low box, with outstretched legs, and a full wine-glass balancing in one hand, and the bottle in the other, giving a ludicrous mimicry of poor Mrs. Mag and her misfortunes.

The acting was sufficiently droll to account for the bursts of laughter which greeted the performance; but as Sir Richard was a liberal host, they would have been accorded, probably, to a less degree of skill in the actor.

When the silence of exhaustion had fallen upon the company, Captain Lymerton, caressing his moustache thoughtfully, said,

"Rivers!—Rivers! are they City people?"

"I should fancy so," said Sir Richard, "judging from the specimen of their friends."

"Rivers," said the Captain again, "very beautiful?"

"Bless me! how can I tell? I gave you the information that she was 'a sweet creetur,' just now; but that is all I know."

"You remember Saint Cyr?"

"Yes."

"Laying siege to a Scotch heiress, isn't

he? Lady Levinge has no end of photographs of him—true," rejoined the Captain, and broke off the conversation, saying that he was tired, and would go to bed; but before he did so, he related to Sir Richard, "in confidence," several particulars which he had learnt from Saint Cyr, with a conviction in his mind that the information would be carried only as far as Lady Levinge's pillow, and there deposited by her unretentive husband.

Very slow was Constance's recovery from her illness; and her mind was borne down by a sense of pain and weariness which depressed her bodily powers, and seemed to forbid their rally. She was pronounced out of danger, and Mr. Johnson recommended her being moved into the ante-room, for a little change; but in the ante-room Eustace had taken up his abode, and for this, or some other reason, Constance declined the proposition, and said she "was not strong enough to walk."

"We will roll you in the great chair," said Lady Yorke, kindly. "Do let us, my dear! I want you to grow stronger. Remember, I cannot be with you without leaving Eustace alone—he has been very patient; but patience is a virtue that is apt to wear out with over-exertion."

Constance flushed painfully.

"Please let me stay here quietly a little while longer," she said. And Lady Yorke had no choice but to consent.

That day the post-bag contained a short letter from Constance to her father.

"Dear papa," it said, "I have been ill, but I am much better; and as I have been a long time with Lady Yorke, I should be much obliged if you would write and propose my return to George Street—that is, if it will not be very inconvenient to you and to Mrs. Rivers."

"Will you not sit with Sir Eustace, madam?" said Constance, that evening; "I can amuse myself with my book quite well; and I feel ashamed of all the trouble and seclusion I have entailed on you."

"Don't be a goose, my dear!—you will tell me next that you are ashamed of having saved Eustace's life. However, I will go to the poor boy for an hour, and give him the pleasure of beating me at chess."

When she joined Eustace, she observed,

"That girl is either very shy, or very coquettish. There can be no doubt that she loves you, or she would not have hazarded her life to save yours; and yet she seems determined to keep out of your way."

"I have never been so vain as to fancy Miss Rivers preferred me," rejoined Eustace; "she has never honoured me with a single look or word which would evince any liking for my society. I am by no means sure that the act she performed that night was not prompted by her affection and gratitude towards you."

"She is a warm-hearted but very timid girl," answered Lady Yorke; "and had she not loved you, she would not have braved the horrors of that night."

"I wish I were assured on that point."

"You had better take the first opportunity of asking her," said his mother, smiling, yet with a little sigh. "It is sure to come," she continued, "some time or other; and I think I can consent to be second in your heart, for the sake of your welfare. It is well that diminutions of happiness should come towards the conclusion of our lives, that death may not find us clinging too closely to ties of earth."

Eustace told her, and believed it at the time, that no one could ever displace her from her supremacy in his affections.

Before Constance had left her bedroom, Eustace was called away on business that detained him for several weeks; and, released from the nervous dread of his presence, Constance recovered her light-heartedness and health. Every day, as her strength augmented, her tenderness and devotion to her hostess increased; but Lady Yorke asked herself whether the impression of Eustace was right, and if indeed her midnight journey had not been undertaken for the sake of the mother rather than of the son.

At Earlscliff, however, the absence of Eustace produced a sensible effect on all the guests, without their being conscious of the cause. It was said by Sir Robert Shirley, when at the Court of the Royal Abbas—immortalized by Collins's Eclogues—that when that potentate came into the divan with a troubled aspect, all trembled at the anticipations of the events of the day. When beaux and belles dropped into the breakfast-room at Earlscliff, they read foul or fair weather in the rounded features of their hostess, and groaned in spirit at the storms or rejoiced at the smiles it prognosticated. The cook was the greatest martyr on the shrine of Eustace—a martyrdom that partook of the torments of Saint Lawrence, and recurred at every meal. At breakfast-time the coffee was too cold, or so weak as to be tasteless, the broiled ham was not crisp, the broiled salmon was luke-warm; at luncheon the hashed venison was tough, and the gravy too much flavoured with wine; at dinner the turbot—got expressly from town by Sir Richard for the delectation of his pretty lady—was woolly, not eatable.

The ladysmaid declared she did not know what had come over my lady. She used to be so sweet-tempered, now she always looked cross, and seemed as if she would scratch her eyes out when she spoke to her.

Sometimes Coralie made an effort to be like her usual self, and was vivacious with the men, and agreeable to her lady guests; but she generally sought to be alone, when her round face would sink into an expression of weariness sad to see. She was furious with Eustace that he had never called since her party; an omission that she would never have noticed in any other man, became a serious crime in her eyes in his case. She longed to see him with a vague, unsatisfied yearning. She felt she *must* see him, must reproach him—how *dare* he stay away from her! Yet, what right, she asked, had she to depend on his coming? What could she want more in life than she had already?—a kind husband, who was only too indulgent; a giant boy of two years old; a beautiful mansion in a deer-park. She was admired by men, and envied by women, but Eustace had regarded her with eyes

> "In whose calm depths the beautiful and pure
> Alone were mirrored."

He saw in her a lovely woman, the wife of his host, but he would as soon have thought of her with love as he would have put his hand into the purse of Sir Richard and purloined his gold.

She knew this, and loved him the more. She was bent on his loving her—*he should*, she declared mentally. When, in the evening, she retired to her sleeping apartment, she dismissed her maid, and stole down the marble steps into the Pleasaunce. His coldness made her half distracted.

"If I could but see him once more!" she

said, as she walked up and down, with quick steps and a flushed face, in the moonlight, keeping within the deep broad shadow flung by the high yew hedge.

CHAPTER XVIII.

"It is not to list to the waterfall,
That Parisina leaves the hall;
It is not to gaze at the heavenly light,
That the lady walks in the shadows of night.
And if she sits in Este's bower,
'Tis not for the sake of the full-blown flower."

HOW quiet everything was in the Pleasaunce! The bright moon illumined the cold statues, which seemed to represent the pause of life rather than its simulation. Diana rested on her bow; Hippolytus, surrounded by the spoils of chase, looked down with clasped hands, as if listening to the accusations of Phædra; a female figure of Contemplation turned her pure face to the quiet sky. All was tranquil except the bosom of Coralie. She looked towards the dark old building, which seemed grander in its depth of shadow, lightened only by the coloured rays which streamed through the windows of coloured glass. These were extinguished, and the lights twinkled in the chambers of the guests and of the servants. She must go back soon, she thought, but instead of doing so she sat down on a seat placed in one of the recesses of the hedge, to try to think quietly. She had sat there one day when Eustace had stood by her side. She had moved her skirt to make room for him by her side, but he had not seemed to notice the invitation. Then, in angry confusion, she had played with her bracelet till the clasp had yielded to her pressure, and the ornament had fallen to the ground. Eustace had picked it up, and kneeling at her feet, he had attempted to reclasp it. The touch of his hands on her arm had thrilled through her frame with an emotion which had astonished her at the time, but which she had not understood nor heeded.

She understood it all now. The thought of his touch, of his head bent down over her arm, of the graceful neck over the back of which the short black curls clustered, increased the tumult in her bosom. She must go to him—if he would not come to Earlscliff. She would go at once. What! walk? eight miles across the country at one o'clock in the morning? Was she indeed going mad! "No one knows it—no one knows of this insanity. I shall get over it in time," she repeated rapidly to herself. She must go back to the house—to bed.

How she loathed the thought of confinement within the four walls! She fancied she could not breathe in the house. How she loathed all the men and women it contained! Most of all, she loathed her kind indulgent husband. "How wicked! how very wicked I am!" she repeated. And then she vowed she would forget Eustace, and never notice him again, and finished by a resolution to send over a formal note to him next day, to borrow a new publication he had procured from London to read to Lady Yorke, as an excuse for compelling him to write, or call, or, at any event, break the dead silence which reigned between them.

At breakfast-time next day one of the party asked if anyone knew where Yorke was? He wanted to ask if he would sell the chestnut horse. Another replied that he was in Yorkshire, looking after some property which had been left to his mother.

"How long will he be absent?"

"I don't know."

And Lady Levinge's heart sank within her,

at first with the thought that he was so far from her; the second idea was more consolatory. If he was away from her, he was also absent from Miss Rivers, whom she was determined he should never marry.

Tossing about on her restless bed, Coralie hit on what she thought to be a bright idea. She would bring Eustace to her feet by making him jealous. He had been so very different from all the men at Earlscliff. His career in the Army had been so brilliant, and he rode so forward in the hunting-field, with such quiet determination to take a line for himself, and never to allow any obstacle to stop him, that his supremacy had been tacitly admitted by all the guests of Sir Richard Levinge. Moreover, Eustace, though naturally stern and hard in his judgments, had learnt, in his attrition with his fellow men, never to lose his self-command.

The only symptom those who knew him best could detect of irritation in his manner, was a deliberate pronunciation of his words, as if each was weighed before it was sent forth. Thus, with quiet, if not soft answers, he turned away wrath, and was geneally considered a sweet-tempered man. He could afford to be sweet-tempered. His "maiden sword" had been so early "fleshed," that he needed not to draw it to prove his valour. Now, though Eustace was pre-eminent in this country house, and in the circle of county families, he had spent his youth in foreign lands, and had never entered the frozen circles of that which is called the best London society. He had never been thrown within its attractions, and knew little, and cared less for its influences.

Saint Cyr, on the contrary, had the *entrée* to all the houses of the *bon ton*.

He was handsome in face and elegant in his figure, had a soft voice, beautiful light curling hair, which, in its texture, resembled more than anything I ever saw the silk wound from the cocoon of the silk-worm. His manners were polished almost to insipidity. Some men said he was *remarkably lucky* at cards,—but then *they* were losers. It was thought that the bets which he generally won were made on the outside edge of honour; but those who thought thus were generally too cautious to promulgate it, and Saint Cyr went on in uninterrupted prosperity, with the reputation of being irresistible with the fair sex, which generally tended to make him so.

With Lady Levinge, however, he had no success. She accepted his homage, and smiled at the worshipper. He had determined to bide his time, and that time had now arrived. A sweet little note on the smoothest of papers, with the most delicate of penmanship, invited him for a prolonged visit at Earlscliff, and there was included in the cover a cordial seconder of the invitation from Sir Richard. Eustace was to be made jealous by seeing the homage he had hitherto received from the fair bevy at Earlscliff, and especially from its mistress, transferred to Saint Cyr. This gentleman was also to be useful to her ladyship in another way, but what might be her schemes futurity must show.

Lady Levinge was determined to give a *fête champêtre* which should eclipse in taste and magnificence all other entertainments of the sort given since Leicester feasted the Queen at Kenilworth. She had some vague feeling that, seeing her the queen of such a court of beauty and grace, Eustace must contrast her with the vulgar belongings of Miss Rivers, and fall down and join the general worship of her charms. To spend some thousands of pounds to obtain such a result, would have seemed to others like "yoking a team of oxen to plant a horse daisy;" but what will not a woman do who loves madly, and loves the wrong person? The idea of this *fête* pleased and occupied her mind, and her husband, family, and guests rejoiced in the improvement of her spirits and temper.

Invitations were sent out to all the neighbourhood, and the 30th of August was fixed, not to interfere with the sports of the gentlemen on the 1st of September. Of course, Lady Yorke, Sir Eustace, and Miss Rivers were included in the number of those to whom cards were sent, and Lady Levinge awaited with some curiosity and more anxiety the answers from Elm Hall. The guests were all expected to appear in fancy costume, or in military and naval uniform. The latter exception was made in favour of the officers of the 15th Cavalry regiment, whose band Coralie hoped to secure, to play in a secluded part of the grounds, where the thick shadows and soft turf might allure stragglers to listen to its spirit-stirring sounds.

Sir Richard, as the thing was to be done, was determined that it should be well done. He caught the infection from his wife, but he, innocent man, cared for no feminine conquest. If Coralie smiled, he was happy. But he was fond of good dinners and choice wines, and determined that those which were provided for his guests should be of the best quality. With a far-sighted prudence, knowing that even Admiral Fitzroy could not prognosticate what the weather would be a month in advance, he provided awnings, which were to be erected in the grounds, sufficiently ample to cover five hundred people, at daybreak on the morning of the 30th, should the day threaten to be wet.

The grounds were in themselves so picturesque, they wanted no embellishment; but few folks really care for rural beauty. Consequently an archery ground was prepared, and a convenient space for croquet was always yielded to the fair and idle guests of Earlscliff.

The cards of invitation caused many a start of surprise, and quickened the beating of many hearts, when they appeared on the quiet breakfast-tables of the sober folks of the neighbourhood. The first feeling of the mammas was pleasure at the thought; but fancy dresses!—only think of the expense!

"Oh! mamma, you cannot think that anything will do for fancy dresses!—you see, any odds and ends——"

"Well, my dears, I don't see how *I* could appear! You will have to ask some one else to chaperone you. Fancy *me* making myself such a *Guy!*"

"Oh! mamma, you might go as Queen Elizabeth, or Bloody Mary, and wear all your jewels."

This last suggestion made mamma deliberate, and the result of female deliberation is well known.

"Oh! Constance, see what I have for you, as well as for myself; and here is a note in the same hand for Eustace—an invitation, also, no doubt."

Constance read the card, and then looked up thoughtfully.

"How very beautiful she is!" was Lady Yorke's commentary on those dark blue fringed eyes and delicate complexion.

"Well, should you like to go?"

"I don't know, madam. I think I should

like it very much, if I could but possess the enchanted ring, to allow me to be there invisible to others, and see without being seen."

"A very singular wish, my dear. I don't think it will be shared by many young folks; though *I* might myself agree with you, for I am anxious to know more about Lady Levinge and the society which Eustace finds so attractive. Yet I am unwilling to leave the seclusion which has been for years my choice and habit. I wonder what Eustace's wishes would be. An early answer is requested. I suppose it is added as a matter of course, and we need not hurry ourselves to reply till I have heard from my son. But, still, Constance, in what costume would you like to appear?"

"I do not know. You see, papa paid a good deal for my mourning, and I think Mrs. Rivers would not like me to have a dress for this party."

"That is true, especially as she and her daughters have of course no cards of invitation." And Lady Yorke thought how provoked that sullen woman would be at the fact of Constance's appearing beautifully dressed in society so far removed in refinement from her own, and determined in her heart that Constance should have one of the most becoming of dresses, without reference to expense.

But Constance could scarcely go without a *chaperon*, and Lady Yorke was not on terms of such intimacy with the mistress of Earlscliff as to ask her to allow Constance to be placed under her charge. The matter was difficult; but Eustace must decide by his wishes what should be done in reference to the invitation. Then, when the answer from Eustace arrived, it appeared that the idea of his mother's re-appearance in society she was so calculated to adorn gave him the sincerest pleasure—of course she and Miss Rivers would accept. He really did not know why Lady Levinge could not let her acquaintances congregate without making such asses of themselves—the men he meant, who were required to appear in fancy costume. He supposed his uniform would spare the trouble and expense of a dress for himself. So the invitations for Elm Hall were accepted.

Eustace told his mother that he should be unable to reach Earlscliff till late in the day, which he regretted, as he should have wished to introduce her himself to Lady Levinge. He would be detained by business; but he trusted to be in time for some of the amusements of the *fête*, and for the enjoyment of seeing his mother take her place amongst the matronage of the county. He was glad that he should see Lady Levinge in a crowd too dense, he hoped, to admit of her plying him with any of the *badinage* he dreaded, on Constance's account, with reference to the unfortunate night adventure. Probably the volatile lady had forgotten the whole circumstance; or, at any event, would be unlikely to recall it in a moment of such excitement and triumph.

END OF THE SECOND VOLUME.

LONDON: PRINTED BY MACDONALD AND TUGWELL, BLENHEIM HOUSE.

www.ingramcontent.com/pod-product-compliance
Lightning Source LLC
Chambersburg PA
CBHW022020240426
43667CB00042B/1012